Better Homes and Gardens®
Container
Gardening Made Easy

Better Homes and Gardens
Container
Gardening Made Easy

BETTER HOMES AND GARDENS®
CONTAINERS GARDENING MADE EASY
Project Editor: Karen Weir-Jimerson, Studio G, Inc.
Contributing Writers: Kate Carter Frederick, Karen Weir-Jimerson
Contributing Designers: Ken Carlson, Bruce Yang; Waterbury Publications, Inc.
Contributing Copy Editor: Fern Marshall Bradley
Contributing Proofreader: Gretchen Kauffman
Contributing Indexer: Donald Glassman
Cover Photographers: Marty Baldwin, André Baranowski, Kritsada Panichgul
Photographers: Adam Albright, Tim Alexander, Craig Anderson, Quentin Bacon, Ball Horticultural Company, Marty Baldwin, André Baranowski, Edmund Barr, Matthew Benson, Laurie Black, Rob Cardillo, Kindra Clineff, Kim Cornelison, Jack Coyier, Degennaro Associates, Erica George Dines, Andrew Drake, Clint Farlinger, Richard Felber, Emily Followill, John Reed Forsman, D. Randolph Foulds, Michael Garland, Susan Gilmore, Ed Gohlich, David Goldberg, Karlis Grants, Justin Hancock, Cynthia Haynes, Doug Hetherington, Richard Himeisen, Bill Holt, William N. Hopkins, Jon Jensen, Mike Jensen, Graham Jimerson, Dency Kane, Mark Kane, Lynn Karlin, Bert Klassen, Pete Krumhardt, Frances Litman, Scott Little, Andy Lyons, Janet Mesic Mackie, Julie Semel Maris, David McDonald, Tom McWilliam, Alison Miksch, Emily Minton, Blaine Moats, Helen Norman, Kritsada Panichgul, Celia Pearson, Mary Carolyn Pindar, Dan Plassick, Nancy Rotenberg, Cameron Sadeghpour, Greg Scheidemann, Dean Schoeppner, Denny Schrock, Joe Schulte, Beth Singer, David Spear, Bob Stefko, Bill Stites, Curtice Taylor, Andreas Trauttmansdorff, Paul Vandevelder, Tony Walsh, Jim Westphalen, Jay Wilde

MEREDITH CONSUMER MARKETING
Vice President, Consumer Marketing: Janet Donnelly
Consumer Product Marketing Director: Steve Swanson
Consumer Product Marketing Manager: Amanda Werts
Business Director: Ron Clingman
Senior Production Manager: George Susral

WATERBURY PUBLICATIONS, INC.
Editorial Director: Lisa Kingsley
Associate Editor: Tricia Bergman
Creative Director: Ken Carlson
Associate Design Director: Doug Samuelson
Contributing Art Director: Bruce Yang
Contributing Copy Editors: Terri Fredrickson, Peg Smith
Contributing Indexer: Elizabeth T. Parson

BETTER HOMES AND GARDENS® MAGAZINE
Editor in Chief: Gayle Goodson Butler
Editor in Chief, Garden: Doug Jimerson
Creative Director: Michael D. Belknap

MEREDITH NATIONAL MEDIA GROUP
President: Tom Harty
Vice President, Production: Bruce Heston

Pictured on the front cover:
top left Group colorful containers in a conga line to make a bold statement.
middle left Kale and ornamental grasses make a stunning fall container pairing.
bottom left Choose plants in different hues of green to create a calming effect.
right Colorful spring-blooming bulbs sprouting from a collection of vintage enamelware make for a thrilling spring container garden.

Copyright © 2012 by
Meredith Corporation.
Des Moines, Iowa.
First Edition.
Printed in the United States of America.
ISBN: 978-0-696-30075-2

All of us at Meredith® Consumer Marketing are dedicated to providing you with information and ideas to enhance your home. We welcome your comments and suggestions. Write to us at: Meredith Consumer Marketing, 1716 Locust St., Des Moines, IA 50309-3023.

Contents

Chapter 1

WHAT'S YOUR CONTAINER STYLE?

Create flower- and foliage-filled containers for your garden that fit your own personal style.

Chapter 2

CONTAINER BASICS

Plant, water, feed, groom. Just a few easy steps allow you to create easy-care containers.

Chapter 3

CONTAINER PLANS

From spring through winter, create gorgeous containers for your yard with easy plans.

Chapter 4

DECORATING WITH CONTAINERS

Amp up the color on porches, patios, and in landscaping with containers.

Chapter 5

PLANT ENCYCLOPEDIA

Choose plants that excel in sun, shade, and in between: perennials, annuals, vines, bulbs.

Shade-loving impatiens and coleus infuse hot color to non-sunny spots. Plant in simple clay pots, which come in many stylish options and sizes.

Petunias offer cascading blooms for window boxes and hanging baskets. These carefree annuals bloom like crazy in hot weather.

Combine annuals and perennials. Here pink geraniums and lime-green lamium rub shoulders in a tabletop planter.

Think out of the box when creating container partnerships. Here Swiss chard, oramental grass, and pansies make a lush (and edible!) combination.

Introduction

Container gardening is the great equalizer. That's because everyone can plant a container garden. You don't have to have a big yard or great soil in order to enjoy a beautiful garden. All you need are containers, potting soil, and plants. You can grow any kind of garden—flower, vegetable, herb—in nearly any kind of pot. In fact, you can even grow plants that you wouldn't think would thrive in containers: shrubs, vines, and even trees.

Everyone can have a container garden

If you dream of having a fabulous garden, your wishes can be fulfilled—all in a container. Containers are the ultimate porch, patio, and garden accessory: They are colorful, portable, and changeable. Whether you are an experienced gardener or just starting out with your first pot of flowers, potted plantings will encourage and feed your creative and nuturing self. As decorative elements in your outdoor spaces, the cheerful and color-filled displays that containers add to your landscape bring pure enjoyment.

Experience plants outside your zone

Containers allow you to enjoy some plants that don't naturally grow in your climate. For example, tropical plants can't thrive in areas with frost, but northern gardeners can enjoy palms and citrus plants in containers on their patios. (You need to take these tender beauties indoors before frost or treat them as annuals.) Likewise, gardeners in humid climates can enjoy dry weather cacti and succulents in containers on their patio tables. Containers truly allow you to garden outside your climate limitations, allowing you to sample an unlimited range of plants. What a luxury to be able to indulge in any type of planting you want!

Low-maintenance gardens

If you are short on time, container gardens are the ultimate easy-care garden. Although contained plants rely on gardeners for their regular watering and feeding needs, you can use one or several strategies to make watering easier. Soil additives that hold water, drip irrigation systems specifically made for containers, and grouping containers with like watering needs are time-saving methods that will adequately quench the thirst of your plants while freeing up your time for other nongardening endeavors.

The easiest way to garden

Growing plants in containers is the easiest way to raise almost any type of plant—from cacti to vines to trees and shrubs. With great potting soil, you'll never have to contend with some of the soil problems that in-ground gardeners face. Potting soil is light and easy to plant in unlike soils that can range from claylike, sandy, or rocky.

When it comes to light requirements in your yard, containers are transportable and can be positioned in the right light for the plantings you choose. For gardeners who want to save their backs and knees, container gardens offer opportunities within reach. Weeds are also less of a problem in containers than in in-ground gardens.

Enjoy containers anywhere

In this book, you'll learn how to create container plantings that can thrive in any type of location: sun, shade, and a combination of both.

For easy-care plantings that bring beauty and versatility to any setting, gardens in containers provide infinite possibilities. All kinds of container gardens can help to enhance your home, set a style, express your personality, tackle your gardening challenges, and improve your quality of life.

CHAPTER ONE

What's Your Container Style?

Create flower- and foliage-filled containers for your yard and garden that fit the style of your yard—and your personality.

16

27

32

left Large containers filled with large plants, such as arbovitae shrubs, make an elegant statement in the garden.
above A succulent-filled bowl makes a beautiful table centerpiece.
below Repurposed galvanized pails and tanks are excellent containers for a wild tangle of ornamental grass.
opposite Cool-weather pansies and primroses surround a center planting of pink tulips.

Define Your Container Garden Style

Containers are so easy to plant. You can create a garden in a pot in just a matter of minutes. Each container reflects style based on the container you choose and the plants you combine in it.

Start with cool containers

The style of the containers you choose helps define the overall style of your garden. Formal containers, such as tall, footed urns, use the classic shapes of the past. For a more casual feeling, employ found-object vessels such as teapots, galvanized buckets, or wooden fruit crates to imbue a cottage-garden feeling. Or choose a neutral container, such as terra-cotta, which offers an earthy palette that can swing from contemporary to classic.

Let color drive your container selection. Glazed ceramic containers come in a rainbow of vivid shades. And plastic and resin pots offer gorgeous hues as well, with the added benefit of being much more lightweight than ceramic (especially helpful when planting large containers that may need transport indoors at the end of summer). Choose a color palette, such as primary colors, pastels, or earth tones. Or choose just one container color, such as bright blue, to create an easy-to-achieve unified look.

Pick the right plants

Of course, a container is just an empty vessel without plants. Which do you choose first? The container or the plant? It can go both ways. Sometimes you find a container that is so beautiful, you buy it just for its good looks. The same holds true for plants. You may fall in love with a gorgeous flowering mandevilla at the garden center and have no container in mind for it. That's not a problem. The matchmaking of containers to plants is the fun of container gardening.

If you are a plant aficionado, let your love of particular plant forms or types dictate what your containers are planted with. For example, you may choose just one kind of plant, such as spiky, textural succulents. When choosing plants for containers, consider the area where your containers will reside: Is it in full sun, partial shade, or full shade? The light in your garden, porch, or patio dictates what kind of plants you need to choose. Also consider the time required for care. If you travel a lot, choose low-maintenance, drought-tolerant plant varieties; they will fare better with occasional neglect.

Design with your heart

Your containers should reflect your favorite things: fragrance, touch, taste, memory. The containers you choose—and the plants that you fill them with—should work together to create the kind of garden that reflects your style, your tastes, and your loves. You can follow an established style (as revealed in the following pages), or you can create a container garden style that is uniquely your own. That's the wonderful thing about gardening—you can be as experimental as you like.

The Classicist:
Formal Style

Formal gardens appeal to homeowners for a variety of reasons: They reflect the style of a period or older home, they work well in small spaces, and they impart a sense of order in a landscape. Formal elements appeal to gardeners who appreciate simplicity and repetition. Additionally, a traditional garden plan is easy to lay out and plant.

Formal container gardens, like formal in-ground gardens, get their stylistic good looks from characteristics that define this style. In general, traditional gardens are symmetrical and balanced. Their design relies heavily on structure, order, and geometry. To achieve these design objectives, think in multiples; repetition is your best friend. If you plant one gorgeous container, plant another one just like it (in an identical pot) to achieve a mirroring, thus traditional, look.

Since structure is such a strong element of traditional style, a traditional container garden is all about pot placement. For example, in-ground formal gardens always have a central axis, such as a path. They also depend on a focal point, such as an accent plant, piece of sculpture, or a bench, to draw the eye inward. You can achieve a similar formal spatial layout by placing containers in a line, square, or circle. For example, in the photo at left, a series of boxwood globes planted in terra-cotta containers encircles a fountain. The simple placement of these containers creates a formal design.

A container can be an element of a formal in-ground garden. For example, many formal gardens use containers as a focal point in the center of the garden. If you don't have space for an in-ground garden, you can create a formal garden using containers alone. Combine traditional plants with classic containers for a formal garden look in an entryway or backyard or on a condo or apartment terrace.

left You can create a formal hedge (in containers!) by planting a group of containers with small shrubs. Boxwoods, clipped into globe, squared, or conical shapes, can create formal structure in patio and garden areas in the same way hedges define space in an in-ground garden.

The Classicist:
Formal Style

(1) Formal containers

One way to achieve a formal container garden is to use classic formal containers; such vessels include urns, bowls, and troughs. These containers can be made from traditional materials, such as stone, concrete, or metal. Or containers are also available in newer, lightweight materials such as aluminum and resin. Containers in formal gardens can be classic urns with large bases to give them height adorned with classical decorative elements such as lion heads or floral motifs. Or containers may be minimalist, such as simple unadorned terra-cotta pots.

(2) Formal container-garden plants

Because structure and order are the dominant style tenets in formal gardens, plant material is often monochromatic: Green and white are popular color schemes in formal gardens. Color takes the back seat in many formal gardens, in part because this allows the structure of the garden to dominate. Traditional foliage plants such as boxwood, yew, and ivy are used heavily in in-ground formal gardens—and in containers as well. These plants are also often malleable—they can change form as a result of pruning or training. In the garden, these plants are used to create structural outlines in beds and borders. And they perform the same job in containers. For example, you can line up a series of containers filled with boxwood orbs to create a hedgelike planting. Or you can train a container topiary ivy to develop a geometric form.

right A conga line of urns makes a beautiful entryway. The heavy-duty iron urns are planted with blue-hued and yellow-tipped trailing succulents at the edges with a large agave in the center.

PLANT IMPRESSIVE

Any plant can adopt the persona of a "traditional" plant, but there are several shrub and small tree species that are specifically associated with this style. Plant them in containers to create green structure. They include:

Yew
Alberta spruce
Boxwood
Mountain laurel
Myrtle
Arborvitae

The Romantic:
Cottage Style

Are you a gardener who thrills to the sight of lots of color, mounds of flowers, and cascades of foliage—all barely contained in the pot they are planted in? Then you are probably a cottage gardener at heart. Whether you adorn your front porch with big, blowsy pots of flowers, hang flower-laden window boxes at every window, or add colorful containers to your garden beds and borders, flower-filled pots can add romantic exuberance to your yard.

You can achieve a cottage-garden feel—in a container—by planting tightly, excessively, and with color and foliage show in mind. Combining plants of all heights, flower sizes, and textures will produce the most magnificent planters. Good container-planting advice is this: Plant a thriller, a filler, and a spiller. In the container, *left*, a good cottage-style thriller might be an old-fashioned favorite such as bleeding heart. (Yes, you can plant perennials in containers!) The shade-loving filler plant could be a mass of dependable

and long-blooming impatiens. And the spiller—try an ivy, such as the variegated, small-leafed 'Glacier'. This trio combination creates a planter that reaches for the sky, tumbles to the ground, and delivers a lot of color in between.

Besides looking lovely to passersby, romantic cottage-garden containers also appeal to wildlife on the wing. For example, hanging baskets packed with red-and-pink fuchsia flowers will bring in hummingbirds; these flying wonders are attracted to the color red. Window boxes planted with zinnias, pentas, and tithonia will lure in nectar-seeking butterflies too.

Consider fragrance when you plant. Many cottage-garden favorites are also sweetly scented, which adds to their romantic allure. Fragrant flowers and foliage include jasmine vine, small rose varieties, and spice-scented dianthus. Position scent-imbued containers near doorways and windows so you can catch sweet whiffs.

opposite Salvaged tin containers, such as old milk boxes, make excellent cottage gardens in a pot. Make sure found containers have drainage holes in the bottom. If not, drill a couple yourself. Most annual and perennial plants don't like wet roots, so drainage is important to plant health. **below left** Mix containers of all styles to create a bountiful cottage feel; galvanized metal, terra-cotta, stone, and wicker can all rub shoulders. **below right** Include a little whimsy in your cottage garden with a topiary animal, such as a foliage-covered strutting rooster.

The Romantic:
Cottage Style

(1) Cottage garden containers

Cottage style embraces the romantic side of gardening, using bits of the past: old-fashioned flowers and unique, repurposed containers. Old stock tanks, salvaged tin buckets, barrels, ceramic crocks, old tea kettles—if the container can hold soil and has a drainage hole, it's fair game for a planting vessel. (If the container doesn't have a drainage hole, you can drill several in the bottom; or simply point a couple nail holes into the bottom to allow water to drain out.) Wood boxes, lined with plastic, make lovely cottage-garden planters and window boxes. Comb your attic, garage, and basement for long-forgotten items that can be planted with flowers and take on new life in your garden.

(2) Cottage garden plants

Romantic containers start with a wide range of plants of different heights, colors, and textures. Old-fashioned flowers, such as roses, hollyhocks, delphiniums, and daisies, can play starring roles. And new, gushy starlets such as cascading calibrachoa and verbena make romantic pot mates.

Nothing increases the romance of a garden like fragrance. Choose plants with scented flowers and foliage to add a sweet perfume to sitting areas or entryways. Many cottage flowers also make excellent cut flowers. (Who says you can't cut container plants to make indoor bouquets?) Daisies, roses, phlox, and black-eyed Susans are just a few of the cottage-garden flowers that also make lovely bouquets.

right A grouping of vintage enamelware pans is packed with small and tall varieties of muscari to create a beautiful color show that lasts all spring. Orange pansies, also cool-weather lovers, add a citrusy splash of color.

ADD FRAGRANCE

Romantic cottage-garden containers smell as sweet as they look. Fragrance-laden flowers include:

Roses
Honeysuckle vine
Hyacinths
Helianthus
Lilacs

A trio of neutral-hue containers creates a contemporary look. Tropical plantings include *Aglaonema* 'Silver Queen', *Angelonia angustifolia*, *Campanula persicifolia*, Chinese evergreen, *Colocasia esculenta*, coleus, *Tanacetum vulgare* 'Silver Lace', and *Tiarella*.

The Modernist:
Contemporary Style

A contemporary container garden gets its modern moxie from many elements. The sleek design and distinctive form of the containers plays an important role. The size, form, color, and textural qualities from blooming and foliage plants add to the look. And finally, the placement and arrangement of the planters are essential ingredients in the overall modern effect.

When it comes to containers, simple is best. Square, rectangular, or rounded containers offer clean lines. The color scheme for contemporary containers can range from earthy tones to organic metallic colors. These subtle colors create a transition from your home's interior to your outdoor landscape.

Tall, upright plants, due to their textural leaves or distinctive growth habit, fit a contemporary garden design. That's why well-defined, symmetrical plantings are often selected for modern containers. Plants add architectural interest and structure to a container. Columnar plants include shrubs such as arborvitae or boxwood, some types of ornamental grasses, and standard or tree forms of shrubs such as butterfly bush or roses. These plants offer vertical lines.

Cascading plants such as burro tail cactus, bacopa, calibrachoa, or ivy also grow in a consistently well-behaved manner and can be used effectively—and artistically—in containers. They offer vertical lines as well.

Spiky plants have a modern feel due to their large symmetrical, pointed leaves. The range in leaf colors is exciting. For example, you can choose agaves with green, blue, or yellow leaves. Phormium has spear-shape foliage in chartreuse, burgundy, or nearly black.

Textural plants such as succulents, including sedums, offer a wide range of leaf shapes and colors as well as a palette of interesting textures and growth habits. From well-branched jade plants to blue-hued echeveria to creeping red-tinged sedums, succulents planted alone or in groups create a contemporary look with ease.

1

PLANT A MODERN LOOK

Choose plants that are textural:

Lamb's-ears
Yucca
Sedum
Barrel cactus
Sago palm
Hens-and-chicks

The Modernist:
Contemporary Style

(1) Modern plantings

An easy way to impose a contemporary feel is through the repetition of the same type or color of plants. In the case of the balcony, *left*, the repetition of white and grayish-green foliage and flowers, in both mounding and cascading forms, creates a modern-looking rooftop container garden "landscape."

(2) Contemporary containers

Contemporary container design can be a little out of the box, or, in this case, *above right*, in the box (but on the vertical rather the horizontal surface). Structure and form are the guiding design elements in contemporary container gardens. Contemporary containers come in all shapes and sizes, and are made from a myriad of modern materials such as resin, polyethylene, fiberglass composites, metals, and hardwoods. Neutral and earthy colors allow the eye to focus on shade and design rather than bold color. Black, white, brown, beige—even brighter earth tones—are ideal color choices for contemporary containers.

(3) Simple style

A minimalist approach to planting can create the most beautiful results. Start with a single specimen of a structurally interesting plant, such as a succulent, *below right*. Aeonium's fleshy leaves change from green to red and curl slightly at the tips: You get a feast of texture and color in the same plant. When it's paired with a simple container, it takes on even more drama. Add a textural mulch of multicolored rock and you've created a quiet, simple planting that will garner lots of attention.

The Individualist: Personal Style

Let your personal passions and interests drive the design of your containers to express your own individual style. Surround yourself with the flowers, containers, and colors that give you joy. Personal style is sometimes referred to as eclectic style, which means you are free of any style constraints. You can mix modern with cottage elements, classic urns with country-style galvanized aluminum. You can't break any rules because personal style has none.

Personal container gardens showcase the gardener's passion. Do you love bright colors? Then pick containers in the hues that make you smile and pack them full with equally bright-blooming flowers. Or are you fixated on just one color? Solitary color themes are easy to create—just choose containers and flowers of one hue. For example, do you like the formality of an all-white garden? Choose white containers (in any style) and fill them with white-flowering and -foliage plants such as bacopa, dusty miller, and petunias. Is blue your favorite color? Then select cobalt blue pots and pack them with the vivid blue blooms of lobelia, fanflower, and blue salvia.

Are you a collector? Then use your collectibles as creative containers. Sprinkle colorful sea glass on top of the soil in pots. Add garden gnomes to containers, letting them peek out from amid the leaves.

Some container gardeners are in love with a specific type of plant: You can make a beautiful and personal garden with just hostas, or just cacti, or just succulents. Animal themes can also be the basis for a personal garden: Cat lovers may add plants that appeal to felines, such as catnip or catmint. Hummingbird fans may fill containers and window boxes with red tubular flowers—the favorite color and flower shape of these winged wonders.

opposite An old stroller gets a new life as a planter packed with succulents. A mix of burgundy, rose, and green succulent texture is created by tightly planting species such as echeveria, hens-and-chicks, and sedum. **below left** A woodland bog garden in a container is a great way to bring nature closer to home. **below right** Gardening with personal style means you can change up the concept of a window box and replace it with three sap buckets filled with small conifers. Add decorative flourishes such as tinsel and ornaments for the holidays.

The Individualist:
Personal Style

(1) Retrofit containers to fit plants

You don't need an arbor or pergola to support a vine. You just need a handmade twig support (or a purchased trellis) inserted into a container so vines can scramble upward. Adding personal touches such as a handcrafted twig trellis or personal artwork makes containers one-of-a-kind pieces of living art.

(2) Colorful containers

Use your container garden to flaunt your love of color. Colorful pots, lined up in a row, add a splash to a lackluster patio or deck. When designing large containers, use large plantings to keep the plants in scale with the containers. Large container plants include ornamental grasses, gerbera daisies, salvias, and coleus.

DECORATE CONTAINERS

Add small statuary, rocks, or other decorations to containers to give them a personal spin. Here are some ideas:

Twigs or wattle
Plates
Silverware
Old gardening tools
Gnomes

Match the color of the plants to the container to create a unified look. Red-hued plants in the large container above include coleus, red salvia, and gerbera daisies.

The Cook:
Kitchen Garden Style

Imagine enjoying fresh produce from your own backyard container garden. It's not a dream! You can grow nearly every type of fruit or vegetable in pots: tomatoes, peppers, onions, herbs, lettuce, strawberries—even fruit trees. In fact, growing edibles in containers is a hot new trend. And it's so easy to do. Even if you have space for an in-ground garden, container fruits and vegetables allow you to grow and enjoy edibles on patios or terraces—and oh-so-close to the kitchen and dining area.

The good news is that many vegetables and fruits may actually do better in containers than they do in the ground. Because so many types of edible plants require well-drained soil, container culture provides an ideal growing medium. Plus, you can position pots in sunny spots in your yard where having an in-ground garden may not be possible.

Start in the early spring with cool-weather crops such as lettuces, greens, radishes, and carrots. If you love fresh greens, sprinkle seeds of these fast germinators into several containers; cut greens when they are a few inches tall. Many "cut and come again" varieties produce more leaves when they are harvested. For a special treat, plant an attractive low bowl entirely with leaf lettuces or greens such as mustard or arugula. When the greens are harvest size, set the bowl directly on the dinner table so guests can clip their own salads directly onto their plates.

To grow edibles in containers, think small. Choose dwarf or small varieties that are better suited for containers. Patio tomatoes are smaller in stature than their larger in-ground cousins. And to satisfy a sweet tooth, plant berries and tree fruits in containers. Strawberries and blueberries grow well in containers. And dwarf varieties of apples, pears, and citrus trees can succeed in containers as well.

opposite Group container-grown tomatoes, peppers, greens, and herbs together to best serve their watering needs. Containers require more watering than in-ground crops, so be vigilant, especially in hot weather. **below left** A bowl of red and green lettuce greens is as beautiful as any floral combination. And edible too. **below right** A kitchen garden can be a simple group of containers packed with herbs and vegetables. Position containers near your kitchen door for easy access to herbs for cooking.

1

PLANT A TEA GARDEN

Fill a container with these soothing, steepable herbs:

Peppermint
Chocolate mint
Rosemary
Chamomile
Lemongrass
Lemon verbena

The Cook:
Kitchen Garden Style

(1) Create an herb garden

Herbs excel in containers too. And you can grow ample amounts of all your favorite flavors. Pack containers with lots of pesto-producing large-leaf basils such as 'Genovese'. For smaller containers, try small-size 'Spicy Globe' basil. Creeping herbs such as thyme and prostrate rosemary make excellent container partners. Keep pots of herbs near the back door so you can step out of your kitchen and snip off leaves for salads, drinks, stews, and pizzas.

(2) Plant tasty combos

Plant vegetable and herb combinations to match your dining preferences. Peppers and basil make excellent additions to Italian or Thai dishes. Tomatoes and cilantro make a good growing pairing for salsa lovers. Tuck oregano or rosemary plants into window boxes or backyard containers so you can snip and clip for recipes.

(3) Terrific tomatoes

Grow colorful small-stature tomato varieties, such as patio tomatoes, in containers on decks and terraces. Tomatoes need full sun, at least 6 hours a day. Provide staking within the container or train tomato plants onto a trellis against a wall to encourage maximum fruit production. Container-grown tomatoes need good-quality potting soil and adequate drainage.

The Specialist:
Theme Containers

For every type of specialty in-ground garden—Asian, rock, or alpine—there is a corresponding way to create the same type of garden in a container. In some ways, specialty gardening is even easier in containers because these gardens are often intricate, complicated, and require a certain level of care. Tiny specialty gardens require less work than a large-scale specialty garden—merely because the space is smaller. The added benefit of creating a small-space specialty garden in a pot is that you can position these special container gardens where they can be admired up close.

Asian gardens, incorporating the clipped-to-precision forms of bonsai tree and shrub varieties, are lovely when created for tabletop decoration. Naturalistic and minimalist, these gardens create detailed landscapes in miniature. Asian garden plants include dwarf conifers, Scotch moss, mondo grass, and weeping tree varieties.

Rock or alpine gardens, which mimic alpine mountainscapes, allow you to grow tiny species of plants that may otherwise be overlooked in a landscape. Alpine rock garden plants include low-growing sedums, creeping phlox, and primula.

Trough gardens use rough containers with a hand-hewn look. Plant them with small creeping species such as sedums and small conifers. Or pack them with spring-blooming bulbs and cool-weather annuals to make an Easter display of bloom you can enjoy for the cool months of spring. You can buy a stone trough or make your own lighter-weight version out of hypertufa, a sand-cement-peat moss mixture. Knot gardens are an ancient style of intricate decorative planting using low-growing plants such as lavender, boxwood, and thyme. It's much easier to create a knot garden in a large container than in a large-scale garden bed.

opposite A springtime trough garden is a beautiful way to concentrate a burst of color in a small space. Lily-flowered tulips, ranunculus, violas, and other cool-weather plants can be packed shoulder to shoulder in a stone or hypertufa trough. As the weather warms, add heat-loving annuals to replace the faded spring blooms. **below left** Make a mini forest using dwarf conifers such as dwarf Alberta spruce, false cypress, and dwarf mugo pine. **below right** Assemble a dreamy fairy garden using small perennials and whimsical miniature garden ornaments.

PLANT A THEME GARDEN

Let whimsy guide you with these themed options:

Mini trough garden
Mini knot garden
Herb garden in a bowl
Zen garden
Tabletop water garden

The Specialist:
Theme Containers

(1) Make a moss village

Luxurious carpeting moss and fleshy succulents make lovely container companions with other shade-loving annuals and perennials, *left*. Low growing and matting, moss also makes excellent filler at the base of planters, skirting around standard tree roses or topiary trees. Try chartreuse Scottish moss, leafy fern moss, or clumping hair cap or cushion moss. Moss thrives in shade but will also thrive in dappled sunlight. Don't place moss in sunny spots.

(2) Try trees or shrubs

Many small-scale trees and shrubs can grow for years in containers. Choose dwarf or slow-growing varieties, *above right*, so that you don't have to transplant often. Standard versions of roses, lilacs, and butterfly bushes also make lovely container subjects. Columnar-shape trees and shrubs make excellent privacy solutions on patios or terraces—try arborvitae, boxwood, and juniper. Spiral-cut or ball-shape evergreen topiaries add personality and style to your garden. Choose juniper, dwarf Alberta spruce, or boxwood.

(3) Set your sights on succulents

A bowl, *below right*, filled with the textural and colorful talents of succulents is so easy to plant and a snap to care for. Pack drought-tolerant succulent species such as echeveria, sedum, kalanchoe, and agave into a shallow bowl. In areas where these plants can't overwinter, plan to bring the container indoors and enjoy as a centerpiece all winter.

CHAPTER TWO

Container Basics

Plant, water, feed, and groom. With just a few easy steps, create easy-care container gardens that will fill your life—and your yard—with color.

42

54

66

left Choose containers to suit yourself and the style of your home. There are no rules other than these: Keep it simple and enjoy the process! **above** Plastic pots make it easier than ever to have portable and pretty gardens. They're also easy to clean—a boon to plant health. **below** A magnificent agave stands out in a lush garden thanks to its architectural strength and the cobalt blue pot that houses it.

The Scoop on Pots

Metal, concrete, terra-cotta, ceramic: There are so many amazing container choices. Whether the container you choose is the main event or a neutral element to show off a spectacular planting, the marriage of containers and plants gives you an endless palette of possibilities.

As a home for plants, containers provide space for roots to develop and plants to grow and flourish. Any container that holds soil can be used for growing plants, from standard terra-cotta pots to ceramic, metal, wood, and fiberglass planters to old shoes, pasta cookers, wheelbarrows, and hollowed-out logs. Key to your garden's success is the container's ability to provide an adequate growing environment for roots, delivering enough space, moisture, nutrients, and air to nurture them.

If you don't already have containers on hand, you'll soon discover that the selection has never been better. You'll find an unlimited array of containers in all materials, sizes, and shapes. They vary in their longevity and ability to provide optimal growing conditions. Ideally, shop where there's a complete selection of containers for you to compare.

The best containers

It pays to buy the best containers you can afford. Poor quality has a way of looking cheap and not lasting. But price does not always equate with quality. Because plants vary in the type of rooting environment they need, you'll want to match the pot to the plants you plan to grow and the environment outside the container. Here's what to look for:

Material Some container materials, such as terra-cotta, are more porous than others. Porous materials are good for plants that prefer soil on the dry side. Nonporous materials are best for plants that prefer wet conditions or for plants that will be placed in hot, sunny, or windy spots. The container should not be so porous that water evaporates rapidly through the container sides. Otherwise, plantings may dry out so quickly that you need to water several times a day.

Drainage A drainage hole or other means of releasing excess water is crucial to a plant's survival. Without good drainage, plant roots can suffocate and die. If a container does not have drainage holes in its bottom, you must create them. Drill one or more holes using a spade bit for plastic or wood, a masonry bit to pierce clay or concrete, or a step bit for metal.

Size The larger the container, the more room for roots and the slower soil dries. However, you need to balance the size of the plant with the size of the pot as well as ensure the pot fits the spot where you plan to place it. Also, some plants prefer cramped roots while others require roomy root space.

- **Large** (16 inches or more in diameter), deep pots offer stability and scale and can host large plants and ones with deep or extensive root systems, such as trees and shrubs. The weight of large pots filled with soil, plants, and water limits their portability.

- **Small** (14 inches or less in diameter) or shallow containers suit small or shallow-rooted plants such as bulbs, succulents, and seasonal annuals. Small containers may become a source of frustration if plants outgrow them, and they will need watering more often.

Durability Well-made containers stand up to weather extremes and watering. Unless waterproofed, wet wood tends to rot and wet metal corrodes. Ultraviolet inhibitors protect plastic from sun damage. Sealants minimize damage to metal from fertilizer salts. Some clay pots are guaranteed frostproof by their manufacturers. Wood, polystyrene (foam), and concrete containers help insulate their contents from weather extremes.

left The pockets of a strawberry pot can hold plants other than strawberries— succulents are one possibility. **above** Containers can be as colorful as the blooms they hold. Broken-glass mosaics are a showy choice. **below** Concrete containers are excellent for large, top-heavy plants such as trees and roses. **opposite** Large wall pots are less likely than smaller ones to dry out between waterings.

Other factors Some container materials, such as concrete, insulate roots from hot and cold temperatures, which is a great benefit in exposed locations. Dark-colored pots absorb heat; in exposed locations, soil dries quickly and roots suffer in the heat and dryness. Water these containers more often. And weight is a movability factor. Lightweight containers can be transported easily (especially important if you need to move pots indoors before frost). But heavy containers, such as concrete and iron, are less likely to topple in strong winds.

Special containers

In addition to terra-cotta, wood, and other traditional pots and planters, you'll find numerous prospects to handle a special job or challenge your imagination.

Self-watering containers feature a built-in reservoir that allows plants to draw moisture as needed, thus minimizing watering chores.

Wall pots are essentially half-round containers with flat backs that fit up against a wall. Strawberry pots offer several pockets for planting along their sides.

Material Matters

Get the most from your containers by understanding the advantages and drawbacks of the materials from which they're made. Materials matter when it comes to watering and other care.

1 Terra-cotta, or fired clay, is either unglazed and porous or glazed and less porous. Heavy when filled with wet soil, it can chip, crack, and break. Because terra-cotta absorbs water, it may crack during freeze-thaw cycles in winter. Low-quality pots easily scratch and chip. High-fired pots are stronger.

2 Concrete, stone, and cast stone excel for durability and elegance. These dense, heavy materials insulate plants from weather extremes, providing a year-round container option, but they are difficult to move. And they are expensive. As concrete and stone age, they develop a patina.

3 Metals, such as galvanized metal, cast iron, and copper, offer versatile style and long life. Shiny metal surfaces usually fade into subtle patinas unless they're powder coated, painted, or polished. Water and fertilizers can corrode metal. Treating the inside of the container with a rust inhibitor can extend the life of the pot. Zinc and aluminum won't rust. Metal pots are nonporous; their weight depends on which metal is used and the size of the container.

4 Ceramic containers are similar to terra-cotta, with the same pros and cons, but are made from a different type of clay. Most are glazed and comparatively heavy.

5 Wood containers range from rugged half barrels to window boxes and patio planters. Minimally affected by heat and cold, wood insulates roots from wide temperature swings. Choose pressure-treated wood, sustainable hardwood, or rot-resistant cedar or cypress. Relatively nonporous, wooden containers can be left outside year-round.

6 Synthetic containers made of fiberglass, plastic, foam, or other resins are lightweight, easy to clean, and nonporous. Coming in countless shapes, sizes, colors, and textures, they have finishes that resemble stone, concrete, or other high-end materials at a lower cost. Fiberglass pots can chip or crack. They are poor insulators, as are thin-walled plastic pots. But plastics can be long lasting. Pots marked UV resistant crack and fade less.

Selecting Plants

Annuals, perennials, trees, shrubs, vines: If you can plant it, it can grow in a container. Choosing plants for containers is as easy as picking up a flat of petunias at the garden center. Or experiment with something larger.

You might shop with a list of favorites in mind, such as the butterhead lettuce and basil that are essential to your summer meals or the dwarf yellow marigolds that work best in those square pots on your front steps. You might head to the garden center with just a color scheme in the back of your mind. Or maybe you just like to be inspired by whatever you find at the store.

As you browse the nursery aisles, you'll find a familiar group of candidates available year after year that have growth habits and requirements well suited to life in your region's climate. These have proven reliable for quick color and good looks, especially in combination with one another. You will also find an wide world of new planting possibilities—a continually expanding array of new and improved varieties. If you let them, these newcomers will inspire your planting schemes and transform your containers from pretty good to gorgeous.

Your ideal plants

Generally, almost any plant can grow successfully in a container, at least for a limited time, as long as you meet its needs for light, water, and nutrients. But determining the best plants for your garden depends on your goals.

Before you start picking out plants, think about what you want to accomplish. Do you seek colorful plantings with the longest season and the least maintenance? Perhaps you wish to dress up your deck or patio with a few big pots of bold foliage for a special event. Or maybe you want to brighten a shady spot in the yard, decorate a dull fence, or transform a small backyard for fall. You'll find plants to address these goals and more.

A trip to your local greenhouse or nursery offers an exciting way to discover ideal candidates for containers. The plant colors, names, and prospects prove dazzling—and dizzying—even for the most advanced gardeners. Enjoy the kid-in-a-candy-store feeling, then step back and apply the guidelines on the following pages to make choosing easier.

opposite, top left An unusual container of purple pineapple lily (*Eucomis* 'Sparkling Burgundy') draws attention. **opposite, top right** Reliable pots of red geraniums and purple petunias add color to a sunny site. **opposite** Switch grass (*Panicum virgatum*) in tall blue pots accents containers of cascading calibrachoa, bright coleus, classic geranium, and *Artemisia stelleriana* 'Silver Brocade'. **above** A pocket planter of violas brightens a rustic wall.

far left This container garden shines on the deck, linking the indoors and outdoors throughout the summer. It includes crape myrtle standards, variegated shell ginger, 'Inky Toes' coleus, and asparagus fern. **left** A well-braced shelf holds wooden tubs of long-season boxwood, purple sweet alyssum, yellow violas, and orange and yellow nasturtiums. **below** Bold mounds of fall-blooming chrysanthemums and leafy kale fill in where spent annuals require replacing late in the growing season. **opposite** Celebrate spring by packing a pot with 'Giant Excelsior' stock, pansies, and pussy willow branches. Enjoy the show while it lasts.

Planting for the Seasons

Regardless of where you live, regardless of the season, there are plants and pots that can add bright color to your yard.

Most people like the idea of an easy-care garden that looks its best throughout the growing season. A large selection of plants is available to make big splashes of spring-to-fall color and form in your containers.

The annuals and frost-sensitive perennials also known as bedding plants carry on and on throughout the growing season, producing reams of blooms, foliage, or both. Petunia, salvia, moneywort, and many others are inexpensive enough to buy in quantity, which encourages experimentation. Use the plants generously, then toss them on the compost pile when they pass their prime.

Long-term prospects

Year-round plantings provide the longest-lasting displays. Many woody plants and hardy perennials will thrive in containers for several years or more as long as the pot is roomy enough to sustain them. Dwarf shrubs and trees work especially well as single-specimen plantings. Select varieties that are at least two zones hardier than your climate and pot them in frost-resistant containers so you can leave them in place over winter. Underplanting with seasonal bedding plants gives the display an extra spark and added color that can last into winter in warm climates.

Temporary tenants

Seasonal plantings jump-start the gardening season in early spring or extend it in fall. Take advantage of the plants that strut their stuff in cool weather by filling pots with them or tucking them around permanent plants. The temporary displays will brighten your world until they peak and die back.

Pansy, viola, dwarf snapdragon, English daisy, and an array of prechilled bulbs (hyacinth, daffodil, tulip) top the list of spring's glorious-but-temporary bloomers. Round out early displays with spring perennials such as primrose, creeping phlox, and forget-me-not. Come fall, cold-hardy pansies, ornamental kale and cabbage, chrysanthemum, and stock, among others, can rejuvenate your waning summer container gardens for a few more pleasureful weeks.

left Take a shortcut to enjoy containers full of spring-flowering bulbs by rounding up presprouted bulbs at a garden center in late winter. **above** In the simplest of garden designs, sculptural agave creates an attractive setting with its singularly striking form. **below** Potted edibles make it easy to have on hand your favorite garden-fresh ingredients, such as tomato, dill, purple basil, and kohlrabi.

Narrowing Your Choices

If you feel overwhelmed by the number of choices at the garden center, simplify the selection by focusing on the practical advantages that different kinds of plants have to offer.

Recognizing a plant's strengths, such as drought tolerance or slow growth, for instance, will help you get the most impact and enjoyment from your container plantings. Look for this information on plant tags, store signage, and in the Plant Encyclopedia at the back of this book. You'll discover gradually which plants give you the greatest return on your investment of effort and money.

Plant types

Knowing the type of plant (think annual, perennial, or shrub) gives you clues about how it might behave in a container. A quick look at plant types will help guide your selections.

Annual plants complete their life cycle in one growing season. They come in a range of colors and forms. Plants that are perennial in warm climates are used as annuals in cooler climates where they're not hardy.

Perennials are a vast group ranging from diminutive groundcovers to large-leaf wonders that return and grow larger each year. Some offer fabulous seasonal flowers; others boast long-lasting colorful or texture-rich foliage.

Shrubs bring sustained color, form, and height to containers. Choose from flowering or evergreen types and dwarf forms.

Trees are the slowest-growing but longest-lived plant group. Dwarf varieties are especially valuable for their form, bringing height and durability to container gardens.

Vines include sprawling, climbing, and clinging plants, both annual and perennial. They're grown for their form as well as for showy flowers or attractive foliage.

Bulbs, including tubers and bulblike plants, offer splendid flowers or tropical-looking foliage for spring, summer, or fall displays.

Tropical plants bring exotic aspects to potted gardens. Many plants grown as annuals are actually tropical or frost-sensitive perennials. Some are commonly sold as houseplants.

Succulents and cacti represent a massive group of plants that are specially adapted to dry, hot climates. Some are cold hardy.

Edibles, such as citrus trees, small fruits, vegetables, and herbs, tantalize senses with their harvestable produce and ornamental aspects. Choose dwarf or compact varieties developed especially for container gardens.

Ornamental assets

When selecting plants, consider their best features: flowers or foliage. Eye-catching flowers grow in an irresistible array of colors and sizes, from the tiny daisies of bacopa to tall, willowy angelonia. Foliage also comes in an astounding variety of colors and shapes. Put it to work as a foil for flowers or grow foliage plants on their own to take advantage of their impressive features. Fantastic containers make use of both flowers and foliage.

Note the plant's growth habit or overall shape. Plants may creep or trail, grow upright, or form a mound. These shapes suggest the best use for the plant in a container.

Be aware of a plant's rate of growth as well as its ultimate size. To ensure a long-lasting composition, only plants with comparable vigor should be grouped in a pot. Otherwise, fast growers such as sweet potato will overgrow slower-paced neighbors such as geraniums.

With help from the plans beginning on page 70, you'll find ways to exploit plants' best attributes in groupings and in single-variety plantings.

Refresh soil in year-round containers annually by replacing the loose soil around the plants' root balls with fresh potting mix plus a dose of slow-release fertilizer.

Soil

Success begins with soil. This mantra applies to all gardeners and gardens. In a container garden, the best soil provides plants with the water, nutrients, and air they need to thrive.

The ideal soil will not come from your yard—garden soil is too heavy, compacts too easily, and drains poorly in pots. Instead, the best soil is formulated to drain well but still hold moisture; it is light enough to make a container portable but heavy enough to keep it from toppling over in a strong wind.

For convenience, use an all-purpose potting mix that includes a blend of ingredients, such as peat, vermiculite, perlite, sand, and bark, suited to most potted plants.

The package will tell you if it's a soilless mix (made primarily with peat, coir/coconut husk, bark, wood chips, or sawdust), which will be lightweight and dry out quickly. A soil-based mix (made with sterilized, garden-variety loam) will be heavier and hold moisture and nutrients longer.

Experiment with both types of mix and a variety of products to determine which ones work best for your plants. You may need different mixes for different types of planters and plantings.

SPECIAL MIXES

A premium potting mix containing slow-release fertilizer and water-holding polymer crystals lessens feeding and watering chores.

Customize a potting mix to suit your plants' needs. For example, make an extra-sandy, well-draining blend for succulents or an organic, compost-enriched mix for edibles. Or enrich and enhance a lightweight, peat-based mix with compost and polymer crystals, making it more moisture-retentive; it will work well for plants that prefer damp soil. Also use this mix in window boxes, hanging baskets, and other containers that dry out quickly.

When blending your own potting soil ingredients, moisten the peat moss and vermiculite with warm water before adding them to the mix. Once saturated, they're easier to manage and blend with other ingredients.

SOIL AMENDMENTS

These ingredients, when included in potting mixes, have specific roles. Customize a mix to suit your plants' needs for moisture and drainage using these materials, compost, sand, and other ingredients.

PEAT MOSS This lightweight organic material soaks up water and nutrients like a sponge.

PERLITE Heat-expanded granules of volcanic ash do not absorb water but help soil drain and resist compaction.

VERMICULITE Flakes of mica (a mineral) expanded by heat absorb water, release it slowly, and keep soil mix porous.

left When planting a container, add enough potting mix to place plants near the top of the container, keeping them at a depth comparable to their nursery pots. **below left** If you discover a plant's roots tightly bound when you remove its nursery pot, gently squeeze the root ball to loosen it and tease loose the roots before planting. **below** Set up a planting area in the shade. After a few days, when plants have recovered from the initial shock of transplanting, move them to their desired location.

Planting

Attention to details at this stage will help ensure strong, healthy plants. Use these techniques and tips to make the process more satisfying.

Plant in place if the container will be too heavy to lift and move when filled.

Before planting terra-cotta or any other porous pot type, soak it in water. A dry clay pot absorbs moisture from soil, taking water away from plants.

Fill a container half to three-quarters full with potting mix. Blend in slow-release fertilizer and, if desired, water-retentive crystals. Top with plain potting mix.

Arrange plants while they're still in their nursery pots. Set them in the container, starting with the largest or tallest and finishing with the smallest ones.

Place the largest plant in the center of the container for a symmetrical design, off to one side for an asymmetrical balance. Rearrange plants until you're pleased with the display.

Just before planting, dip each plant's root ball in a solution of water and root stimulator formulated for transplants (available where garden supplies are sold).

Remove one plant at a time from its nursery pot, starting with the largest. To dislodge a large plant from a nursery pot, gently lay the pot on its side and press firmly on it with your foot. Roll the pot to the opposite side and repeat the process. Then slide the plant out of the pot.

To plant, set the plant in the container and add potting mix around the root ball. Set smaller plants in place. Fill in between plants with soil mix, without packing the mix.

If you wish to plant seeds, sow them directly in a container filled with potting mix. Follow planting instructions on seed packets.

Leave 2 inches between the top of the soil mix and the rim of the container for water and mulch.

After planting, moisten the potting mix thoroughly (until water runs out the pot's drainage hole).

THE DRAIN GAME

Every container must provide drainage, giving excess water an escape route.

SCREEN If a container's drainage hole is large, cover it with screening, newspaper, or a coffee filter to prevent soil from leaking out.

GRAVEL If a container has no drainage hole and you prefer not to drill one in it, create a drainage area using a 2-inch layer of gravel.

LINER When lining a container with landscape fabric or plastic, cut drainage holes in the liner.

left Water-holding polymer crystals absorb moisture and dissolved nutrients, then gradually deliver them to plants' roots as needed. Add crystals to potting mix before planting. **right** Collect and use rainwater on plants whenever possible. Plants will be affected if the water supply at your home is hard (contains mineral salts) or softened. **below** Hand-watering with an adjustable watering wand attached to a garden hose helps control the flow with less waste and directs water into the soil instead of on foliage.

Watering

Consistent, routine watering is vital to plants' health, especially when roots can't seek out moisture because they're confined.

Containers usually require watering daily during summer or every two or three days during cooler periods, unless nature handles it for you. Hot, dry weather and small pots can necessitate twice-daily watering.

Plants suffer from too much water as much as from too little. Determine if a container garden needs water by poking your finger into the soil up to the second knuckle. If the soil feels dry, it's time to water. Check pots daily.

Saturate the potting mix thoroughly. Excess water should drain away from the containers. Soil sours, roots rot, and root-killing mineral salts build up in a container that drains poorly.

If a soilless mix dries out completely, rewet it by standing the pot in a large vessel of water overnight.

Watering early in the day is best. It allows plants to soak up what they need before afternoon heat causes excessive evaporation. Watering in the evening can leave moisture on foliage and promote disease.

Use a watering can to water only a few containers. Group pots and water them all at once.

Using drip irrigation set up on a timer takes the work out of watering. A drip system also saves water by delivering it near plants' root zones with as little evaporation and runoff as possible. Check the system seasonally, especially in hard-water areas, to make sure the timer works and lines are not clogged or punctured.

Self-watering pots feature a built-in reservoir that delivers moisture to the soil. They require watering less frequently. Water-holding mats fit into the bottom of hanging baskets and other containers, wicking moisture into the soil.

IRRIGATION MADE EASY

A simple-to-install drip irrigation system can be customized to suit your garden and target your thirstiest plants.

DRIP IRRIGATION A drip system supplies water to containers via tubes branching from a main line.

EMITTER Place one emitter—attached to flexible tubing—in each container, even a hanging basket.

AUTOMATIC TIMER An automatic timer turns a drip irrigation system on and off, handling the job for you.

Feeding

High-performance plants need nutrients to produce vigorous foliage and bright blooms. Regular fertilizing helps keep container plants healthy.

Gradual-release plant food, blended into a potting mix before planting, offers an easy way to feed container plants continuously. The coated granules release nutrients slowly, usually over three to nine months, depending on the product.

If you use a standard potting mix that does not already include fertilizer, add gradual-release fertilizer according to package directions. Additional granules can be scratched into the soil mix later as a nutritional boost if needed.

Water-soluble plant food is an alternative. Make a solution of plant food and water, sprinkle it on the soil, and reapply it regularly throughout the growing season.

The plant food label indicates—in a series of numbers separated by dashes—the balance of the major nutrients it supplies: nitrogen-phosphorus-potassium. An all-purpose, 14-14-14 fertilizer gives plants the primary nutrients they need to thrive.

Some plants need feeding more often, including those in close quarters or growing in a soilless mix. Fast-growing, vigorous plants are also more hungry.

Edible plants and long-term plantings benefit from organic fertilizers that enrich soil and improve its structure. Organic fertilizers include compost, rotted manure, fish emulsion, and kelp products.

Plants show signs of nutrient deficiency particularly in their foliage, alerting you to their need for fertilizer. Clues include pale or discolored leaves, weak or slow growth, and smaller leaves and flowers.

Taper off plant food as the end of the gardening season approaches.

opposite left Sprinkle granulated fertilizer into potting mix before planting. ***opposite, above right*** Fertilizer leaches through potting mix more quickly in terra-cotta and unglazed earthenware pots than in plastic or glazed pots. ***opposite right*** Give plants a boost at planting time with a water-soluble transplant fertilizer. ***above*** Check package directions for correct fertilizer amounts. More than recommended amounts can be harmful to plants.

Mulching

Mulch is a funny word, but the stuff has a serious job. Mulching is not necessary, but it benefits your garden and keeps your plants healthy.

Mulch prevents soil from washing out of pots and splashing on foliage when you water plants.

Mulch insulates soil and plant roots, helping them keep cooler during the hot days of summer.

Organic mulches, such as cocoa shells and chipped or shredded bark, decompose gradually and add nutrients to the soil mix. Ornamental mulches, including pebbles, shells, and recycled glass, are pretty and effective materials.

Mulch deters squirrels, slugs, and other critters from pestering container plantings. Squirrels won't bother digging in gravel or medium- to large-bark mulch. Slugs will avoid any gritty mulch.

How to mulch

In spring, after rain or watering, top the soil with a 1- to 2-inch layer of mulch. Apply it loosely and evenly; avoid compacting mulch and piling it up around plant stems.

Take advantage of the ornamental value of many mulches. Crushed recycled glass, polished river stones, marbles, and flat glass drops come in a multitude of colors. They glisten when wet and reflect sunlight. Terra-cotta spheres and seashells are especially eye-catching.

Mix and match plants and mulches to find the most effective and pleasing combinations. For example, organic nutshells and fragrant cocoa shells work especially well in edible gardens; herbs and alpines have a proclivity for fine gravel.

opposite, above left A layer of amber recycled glass makes a beautiful soil topper for a single succulent in a pot. *opposite left* Small shells add a textural touch to terra-cotta containers planted with ornamental grass. *opposite, above right* Cocoa shells make a beautiful fine mulch for small plants such as coleus or herbs. It has another attraction: It smells like chocolate. *opposite right* Terra-cotta spheres look beautiful while protecting the soil's moisture level. *right* Add pea gravel to the top of a container to add texture to potted herbs.

AFTER

BEFORE

left A quick makeover revives a tired container. A dying geranium and spindly petunias are removed, leaving a healthy New Zealand flax. Then African daisy, heuchera 'Dolce Key Lime Pie', and wood spurge 'Efanthia' are added to refresh the planting. *above* Deadheading entails pinching or cutting off flowers that have finished blooming. *below* Revitalize plants with weak growth by lifting them from the pot, loosening the roots, replacing the potting mix, and replanting.

Grooming

It takes just a few minutes a day to keep container gardens healthy and vigorous. Combining grooming and watering in a routine also gives you an opportunity to spot any disease or pest problems early. Follow these steps to accomplish basic maintenance of your plants.

Deadheading

Remove flowers as soon as they begin to shrivel, fade, or otherwise appear spent. You can snip them off with your fingers or use pruners.

Pinching off spent flowers also helps prevent annuals from completing their life cycle and producing seeds. This keeps them blooming longer.

While you're at it, remove any discolored or damaged foliage. Snip off and compost. If it looks like the foliage is diseased, destroy it rather than composting.

Pruning

Snip back fast-growing or untidy plants that show signs of unruliness or unattractive bare stems.

Trim a plant for a better shape in graceful proportion to the container and any planting companions. Cutting off foliage reinvigorates the plant and helps produce more growth.

Prevent annuals from becoming scraggly or overgrown by midsummer, trimming 1 to 2 inches from them every other week. If plants become scraggly and bloom less, cut them back by one-third to one-half; then fertilize the plants and watch them rebound quickly.

Replanting

By late summer or early fall, when some plants have passed their peak and appear bedraggled, it is time to replace them. Use a hand trowel to carefully lift a declining plant from its container and replace it with a new one. For example, cool-weather annuals often wilt in summer's heat, so replace them with heat-loving varieties.

Long-term plantings need rejuvenating too. After two or three years, remove the tree, shrub, or perennial from the pot. Trim as much as one-third of the larger roots, especially those circling the root ball or tangled in tight masses. Loosen the root ball. Replant in a pot at least 2 inches larger with fresh potting mix.

Pests & diseases

Look for signs and symptoms of pests or diseases, such as disfigured or discolored foliage or visible insect pests. Take action right away.

Diagnose the problem accurately before taking steps to remedy it. Ask your local extension agent for help diagnosing the problem.

Treat the problem with the correct remedy. For example, not all insects are destructive in the garden. Treat only for those insects that are causing damage.

Handpick pest insects and drop them into a cup of soapy water. Or blast them off leaves with forceful spray from a garden hose. Remove and discard affected plant parts.

far left An iron plant stand uses vertical space to display a collection of small pots. The arrangement makes it easy to tend the garden. **left** A tall plant stand provides a decorative means of displaying small container gardens and keeping them within easy reach. **below** Pot feet promote plant health by lifting containers enough to allow excess water to drain away easily and more oxygen to reach plant roots.

Pot Holders

Giving your container garden a lift—literally raising it off the ground—has practical advantages. It provides good drainage and protects surfaces.

Pot feet add to the decorative charm of a container garden. Elevating a pot using pot feet raises it enough to facilitate drainage. Using pot feet also allows air circulation under the pot and prevents staining of the surface beneath.

Placing a saucer under a pot catches excess water and helps prevent surface staining too. Pour excess water out of a saucer—only some water garden plants benefit from standing with their roots submerged.

If a pot lacks a drainage hole and drilling one isn't an option, use it as a cachepot—a decorative holder—instead. Set a planted pot in it, elevating the inner pot with a 2-inch layer of gravel, pot shards, or styrene packing materials to allow drainage. Empty any excess water occasionally.

Set the stage

Showcase your container gardens by staging them at different levels for greater appeal.

Choose a plant stand that will weather the elements outdoors. A stand with multiple shelves and a tiered design enables you to display a variety of containers and even store gardening tools.

Make sure elevated containers are stable. Beware of placing large or heavy containers on the highest shelf of a tiered stand, making it top-heavy. A tall or tiered plant stand may need to be anchored to an adjoining wall to stabilize it.

Match the accessory to the task. The extra weight of an iron plant stand or an anchored plant shelf can help keep a pot upright on a windy day.

HOLD IT!

Consider an array of options for elevating your container gardens. Wrought-iron accessories prove weatherworthy and handsome.

A plant stand gives legs to a container, boosting its drainage ability as well as its visibility.

An iron pot holder, fastened to an exterior wall, secures a window-height planter. It's like a mini window box.

Some plant stands can be moved indoors with your potted plants.

Summer & Winter Care

Planning a summer vacation? Remember your container gardens and make arrangements to help them survive while you're away for an extended period. While you're at it, think ahead to cold-season protection and safeguard your investment in plants and pots.

Plants should fare well for a long weekend as long as you leave them well watered.

Prepare for a longer getaway by grouping plants close together, out of direct sun and wind (under the eaves of the house or garage, for instance).

Ask a neighbor or friend to check on your container gardens while you're away and water if necessary.

Set pots on a 1-inch layer of stones or gravel inside large saucers or tubs. Pour water into each reservoir until it reaches the pot's bottom.

Remove fading flowers and harvest mature and nearly ripe vegetables and fruits to reduce the drain on plants' resources.

Plan way ahead: At planting time use self-watering containers, drought-resistant plants, and a potting mix that contains moisture-holding crystals. Your container gardens will be less dependent on you for water.

Cold-season protection

Where freezing weather threatens plants, protect them and your pots from the ravages of winter.

Most containers will be at risk if left outdoors unprotected during winter. Moisture from rain or snow held in a pot can freeze and expand, cracking or breaking the vessel.

Weatherproof containers such as resin or plastic can be left outdoors year-round, but they require good drainage to complete their job effectively.

Before planting a year-round pot, line it with bubble wrap to help protect the container from damage caused by wet potting soil freezing, expanding, and pressing on it.

Move containers off a deck or other exposed site and set them in a garage, shed, or more sheltered part of the landscape.

In Zones 4 and colder: Move tender plants indoors for the winter.

Save valuable trees, shrubs, and perennials by lifting them from containers and transplanting them into a garden bed in late summer or early fall.

In Zones 5, 6, and 7: Protect potted trees and shrubs by wrapping the pot and plant in a winter coat made of layers of bubble wrap and burlap. Secure the coat with twine.

Keep leftover soil mix slightly damp throughout the winter months so it's easy to use the following spring.

opposite, above left Watering kits with timers, such as the Green Genius system, work while you're on vacation. *opposite left* Snow-filled pots look pretty, but this is one of the worst ways to leave them at the end of the gardening season. They'll be vulnerable to damage from frost, ice, and freeze-thaw cycles. *opposite, above right* Leave well-watered potted plants in a shaded place with saucers under them. *opposite right* Glass watering mushrooms or globes slowly drip water to plants' root zones.

Portable Pots

Large, bulky pots can be heavy, especially when filled with soil and plants. Use these tips to lighten the load and move pots more easily without injuring yourself.

Plan for mobility. Take advantage of lightweight and portable containers. Made of polystyrene, resin, or fiberglass, they resemble heavier terra-cotta, stone, or concrete.

Choose a lightweight potting mix, especially when the container's weight poses an issue, such as a larger or permanent planter on a balcony or rooftop.

Lightweight pots and tall containers with narrow bottoms need a weighted base to stabilize them and prevent tipping.

Lighten a large container by reducing its volume. Fill the bottom third (or less) of it with styrene packing pieces secured in a plastic shopping bag.

Placing bricks or large stones in the bottom of a lightweight container will help stabilize it but won't improve its mobility.

If you can't lift a potted planting, it's probably too heavy to place on a railing, bracket, or hook.

Move it!

Rolling plant stands and other caddies with casters make moving heavy containers a breeze. Plant caddies also remedy the problem of excess moisture collecting under pots and damaging the surface beneath.

Casters roll easily across a hard surface. Move a pot across ground, gravel, or another soft surface by sliding a tarp or sheet of heavy-duty plastic under the container and dragging it.

Move container gardens before—not after—watering. Watering adds a considerable amount of weight, especially if you are using a mix that contains water-holding peat moss.

above Keep containers liftable by using lightweight soil mixture with sphaghum peat moss. *opposite, above left* Sliding a pot around on a patio, deck, or other hard surface can mar the surface and damage the pot. Use plant stands on casters or caddies to avoid problems. *opposite, bottom left* A large seasonal container requires less potting mix if you fill the bottom of it with pinecones, plastic water bottles, or overturned nursery cell packs. *opposite, above right* Use the leverage of a two-wheel dolly or hand truck to shift and cart hefty pots. *opposite right* A pot lifter turns the chore of hoisting a heavy pot into a quick-and-easy task for two.

left Ideally, your potting area will be located within convenient reach of garden areas and sheltered from afternoon sun. **above** Fall cleanup includes emptying and cleaning containers before storing them. When the gardening season returns in spring, you'll be ready to grow with clean pots. **below** A garden carryall—whether a repurposed vintage milk bottle carrier like the one shown, a bucket, or another holder—keeps hand tools and other supplies handy and portable. **opposite** A stiff brush helps remove soil and debris, preventing the spread of disease to new plants.

Clean & Tidy

An efficient workspace, where you can store clean pots as well as other potting supplies, makes it easier to plant and maintain container gardens.

A well-equipped potting bench fulfills a gardener's fantasies by keeping essential gear organized, within easy reach, and tidy. Keep personal items such as gloves, hats, and sunscreen nearby and ready for use.

Built at counter height, a potting bench provides a sturdy work surface that doesn't require you to stoop or crouch while planting. A bench with shelves above and below the work surface makes an efficient arrangement.

If a potting bench includes a small sink or other water source, it makes cleanup a snap.

A high-quality, well-constructed bench made of cedar or other weather-resistant wood that's screwed or bolted together will last longer than pine or another bargain model.

Place your potting bench in a sheltered area, under an eave, or in a garage or shed.

A small outbuilding dedicated to potting plants will prove a useful asset in any garden.

Build a potting shed or bench using plans, a kit, or the services of a carpenter. Or find ready-made options available from building supply stores, mail-order sources, and online vendors.

Clean, oh clean

Use a stiff brush to clean pots. A wire brush helps remove mineral deposits and stains, but it can scratch and ruin some pots. A scouring pad made for kitchen or grill cleaning can scrub without scratching. Test any scrubber on the pot's bottom first to see if it leaves scratches.

Use a splash of white vinegar on a scrubber to remove white, crusty mineral deposits on clay or other porous pots.

Use a sprinkle of baking soda on a plastic scrubber to scour synthetic pots.

Disinfect pots by soaking them for 24 hours in a solution of 9 parts water, 1 part bleach, and a squirt of liquid dish detergent; and then scrub.

CHAPTER THREE

Container Plans

From spring through winter, create gorgeous containers for your yard and garden. With plant lists and growing tips, these container plans are a snap to plant.

86

91

97

Essentials

Container: 4-foot-long window box

Light: Sun

Water: When soil begins to feel dry

Ingredients

A. 4 yellow lantana

B. 5 purple (annual) verbena

C. 2 white pentas

D. 4 creeping zinnia *(Sanvitalia speciosa)*

E. 3 purple globe amaranth *(Gomphrena globosa)*

F. 4 zinnia ('Profusion White')

G. 5 yellow French marigold

H. 3 rose purple calibrachoa

I. 3 pink-flowering white gaura

J. 7 curly parsley

Notes

Provide plants that serve all of butterflies' life stages. They need places to lay eggs and form a chrysalis; leaves, stems, and buds for caterpillars to feed on; and nectar for adults. Red, yellow, orange, pink, or purple flowers tend to attract the most adult butterflies. Parsley, carrot, dill, fennel, and nasturtium are favorites of caterpillars, depending on the butterflies common in your area.

GREENER GARDENS

Refrain from using toxic pesticides and herbicides near your Butterfly Banquet. They're lethal to butterflies as well as bees, lady beetles, and other beneficial insects.

Butterfly Banquet

Turn the space outside your window into an irresistible stop for nature's brightly colored winged beauties by offering their favorite foods in a collection of easy-care flowering plants.

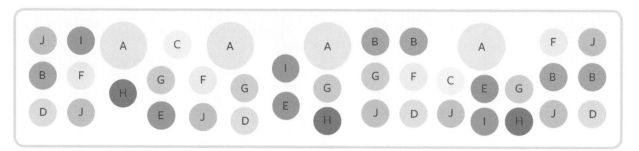

HERE'S HOW...

1 Prepare the window box

Use a plastic liner to help preserve the integrity of a wooden window box. Set the potted plants in the liner to determine a pleasing arrangement: Place taller plants in back; drape arching plants over edges.

2 Fill the liner with potting mix

Unpot the plants and nestle their root balls into the potting mix. Cover the root balls with potting mix, leaving an inch of space below the box's rim to allow for watering.

3 Help plants get off to a good start

Spread ½ inch of mulch (shredded bark or cocoa shells) over the soil. Water thoroughly, until water begins to drip from the container's bottom. From then on, water when the soil begins to feel dry.

Rise & Shine

If the gardening season doesn't come soon enough for you, pots of flowers will make your dreams of spring come true in a snap. Welcome early spring with plantings of flowering bulbs and cool-season annuals that can handle the typical temperature swings and light frost of the season.

Essentials

Container: 18-inch terra-cotta pot

Light: Part shade to sun

Water: Keep soil damp. Spring rains may handle the job for you.

Ingredients

A. 8 white-and-pink tulip (*Tulipa* 'Diamond')

B. 3 Moroccan toadflax (*Linaria maroccana* 'Fantasy Speckled Pink')

C. 8 pansy ('Panola Pink Shades')

D. 5 white tulip ('Diana')

Notes

Spring-flowering bulbs such as tulips have a brief season of bloom. When the flowers have finished, gently tug the bulbs from the container and replace them with early-summer-flowering bulbs such as calla lily.

BHG TEST GARDEN TIP · INSTANT SPRING

Most garden centers offer selections of ready-to-grow prechilled bulbs (daffodils, tulips, hyacinths) and cool-season annuals in early spring—perfect for grouping in pots. Buy them in early stages of development, with their green tips barely protruding from the soil, to get the most and longest enjoyment from them.

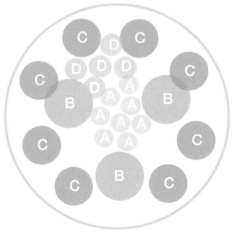

Essentials

Container: 24×15×8-inch lightweight concrete trough

Light: Part shade to sun

Water: Keep soil damp. Spring rains may handle the job for you.

Ingredients

A. 4 yellow tufted California poppy (*Eschscholzia caespitosa*)

B. 3 pink dwarf snapdragon

C. 6 *Felicia heterophylla* (pink; blue) ('Spring Merchen Mix')

D. 6 pink tulip ('Elegant Lady')

E. 4 Persian buttercup (yellow; pink) (*Ranunculus asiaticus* 'Bloomingdale')

F. 4 purple pansy

G. 2 annual candytuft (*Iberis amara*)

Notes

As an alternative, plant a trough with a single variety of prechilled bulbs for big impact. Once the bulbs have finished blooming, toss them on the compost pile and replant the container with summer-flowering annuals.

Mixed Company

This garden's diverse plantings and roomy container create a spring display as pretty as any full-size garden—just the ticket for lifting spirits from late-winter doldrums. Include plants that may not ordinarily grow in your region such as Persian buttercup, which does best in cool climates, and enjoy a blissful out-of-climate experience.

Seasonal Changeouts

Plant a container garden that goes with the flow, changing with the seasons. Start with a core group of slow-growing, long-lasting foliage plants that will stay put from spring through fall. Combine them with seasonal bloomers, then refresh the plantings periodically as they fade.

Essentials

Container: 36×48-inch concrete planter
Light: Sun to part shade
Water: Keep soil damp.

Ingredients

Core plants

A. 3 ruby grass (*Melinus nerviglumis* 'Pink Champagne')

B. 3 *Alternanthera* ('Purple Knight')

C. 3 chartreuse licorice ('Limelight')

D. 3 heuchera ('Dolce Creme Brûlée')

Spring container (shown at left)

3 purple salvia

6 purple viola

6 purple pansy

Summer container

3 variegated orange-green-white coleus

3 wax begonia 'Cocktail Rum'

3 purple plectranthus

Fall container

3 flowering kale

3 bronze-flowered chrysanthemum ('Blushing Emily')

3 ornamental cabbage

Notes

The seasonal plantings will excel for a time, depending on the weather. When you're ready to change parts of the display, relegate the passé plants to partly shady parts of the garden if you can't bear to compost them.

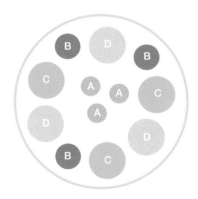

Essentials

Container: 12×36-inch tiered wire basket.

Materials: Landscape fabric or moisture-holding liner and moss

Light: Sun

Water: Keep soil damp.

Ingredients

A. 6 strawberry ('Sequoia')

B. 6 strawberry ('Quinault')

C. 6 strawberry ('Ozark Beauty')

Notes

Line each basket to hold in soil and moisture. Plant the crowns (where roots and stems meet) just above soil level. Feed plants every two weeks with a high-phosphorus fertilizer to prompt flowers.

BHG TEST GARDEN TIP
STRAWBERRY YIELDS FOREVER

You'll find varieties of strawberries for different seasons and regions. June-bearing plants offer a short, intense crop in the spring. Everbearing plants produce fruit intermittently from spring into fall.

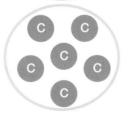

Strawberry Short Stack

Strawberries' shallow roots make them ideal for containers. Keeping plants within easy reach and in a space-efficient planter stacks up to luscious pleasures you can eat right out of hand.

Bucket of Blooms

Set off floral fireworks with an explosion of red, white, and blue summer-flowering annuals. Plant by mid-May in order to enjoy fully blooming plants in time for an Independence Day celebration.

Essentials

Container: 12-inch galvanized bucket
Light: Part shade or shade
Water: Keep soil damp

Ingredients

A. 1 begonia ('Baby Wing White')
B. 1 lobelia ('Laguna Sky Blue')
C. 1 begonia ('Nonstop Deep Red')

Notes

Unless nearly mature and fully flowering when you buy them, the fastest-growing young annuals take about six weeks to reach their blooming stage. Space plants from cell packs or small (2- to 3-inch) pots about 4 to 6 inches apart, giving them room to fill out.

BHG container BASICS — EXTEND THE SEASON

Easily convert a galvanized metal container such as a bucket into a planter by poking at least one hole in its bottom to allow for drainage. Use an awl and hammer to puncture the metal.

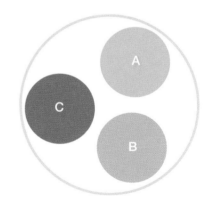

Essentials

Container: 6-foot-long cedar window box

Light: Part shade or sun

Water: Keep soil on the dry side.

Ingredients

A. 2 upright juniper

B. 4 agave

C. 2 burro's tail *(Sedum morganianum)*

D. 5 ghost plant *(Graptopetalum paraguayense)*

E. 2 giant echeveria

F. 2 stonecrop (creeping variety)

Notes

The hardiness of succulent plants varies. Some can remain outdoors year-round in Zones 7 and warmer areas. Many must spend winter indoors in order to survive.

BHG container BASICS — SUCCULENT FACTS

These plants have evolved to withstand periods of little or no rain by storing water in their fleshy leaves or bulbous roots. If you water succulents too much, the plants will rot.

Long-Term Lease

A massive window box pumps up a home's curb appeal by adding charm with a succulent and evergreen twist. The best window boxes can be viewed and admired from the street.

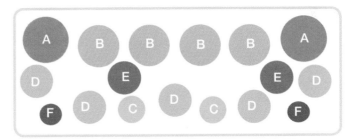

Raising Standards

Elevate your garden style with shrubs trained to stand out. Roses reign supreme as a favorite among those grown and pruned into standards, or tree forms. Make it easy by starting with a ready-made rose standard.

Essentials

Container: 18-inch terra-cotta pot

Light: Sun

Water: When soil begins to feel dry

Ingredients

A. 1 pink miniature rose standard

B. 8 pink vinca

C. 8 pink wax begonia

Notes

Roses grow best in full sun with 1 inch of rain per week (or 1 gallon of water). Use a water-soluble fertilizer once a week or granular food monthly. Alfalfa pellets worked into the soil are an organic source of nitrogen and can be used as a slow-release supplement in spring. Use pellets that are not feed-grade so your rose food doesn't end up as snacks for rabbits.

PLANT SWAP — ALTERNATIVE PLANTINGS

A range of flowering shrubs, dwarf evergreens, tropicals, and others adapts beautifully as standards and have become widely available at nurseries and garden centers. They include lilac, hydrangea, butterfly bush *(Buddleja)*, dwarf blue spruce *(Picea pungens* 'Globosa'), lantana, and citrus.

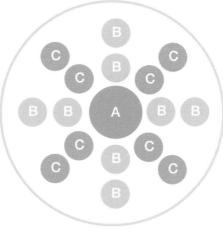

Essentials

Container: 18-inch terra-cotta standard pot

Light: Sun

Water: When soil begins to feel dry

Ingredients

A. 1 boxwood topiary

B. 6 pink vinca

C. 5 lavender lobelia

D. 5 dichondra ('Silver Falls')

Notes

Many gardeners shape boxwood with an electric hedge trimmer, but it's best to pinch or clip the branch tips. Trimming each stem at the junction of another stem encourages better form as new growth develops naturally from several places. Trim boxwood in early spring and late summer.

TOPS IN TOPIARY

Boxwood's ability to handle shaping makes it a classic choice for topiary forms. Start with a preformed shrub in a shape you desire, such as a lollipop or cone. Choose a slow-growing, cold-hardy variety such as 'Little Gem' if appropriate in the climate where you live.

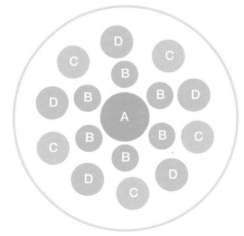

On the Ball

Choose boxwood to anchor a potted garden with its sturdy evergreen appeal. As a shrub, boxwood offers versatility of form and a foil for color contrasts. As living sculpture, it has been called the world's oldest garden ornament.

Butterfly Ball

A dwarf variety of butterfly bush proves perfect for a sustainable container garden. Leave it in the container from year to year, but experiment with combinations and change out the other plants. If you like, include other plants that attract butterflies.

Essentials

Container: 18-inch terra-cotta pot with pot feet

Light: Sun

Water: When the soil feels dry

Ingredients

A. 2 blue salvia ('Evolution')

B. 1 canna ('Bengal Tiger')

C. 2 calibrachoa ('Mini Famous Double Blue')

D. 1 butterfly bush (*Buddleja* 'Blue Chip')

Notes

Dwarf or slow-growing varieties of shrubs and trees make ideal candidates for container gardens. In warm climates, they'll typically thrive for several years before outgrowing the pot. Refresh the soil annually. When the soil dries out at increasingly shorter intervals, transplant the shrub or tree into the garden.

BHG TEST GARDEN TIP

NURSERY TIME

Economize by purchasing immature shrubs and small trees in 1-gallon or smaller pots. Nurture them in container gardens for a year or two before giving them a permanent home in the landscape.

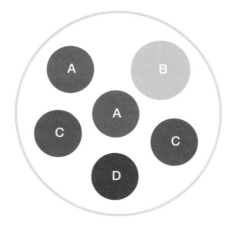

Essentials

Container: 18-inch terra-cotta bowl

Light: Sun

Water: Allow soil to dry between waterings. Water sparingly through winter months.

Ingredients

A. 1 giant echeveria

B. 5 echeveria ('Silver Spoons', 'Perle von Nurnberg', and *E. shaviana*)

C. 10 golden sedum

Notes

Plant succulents in a potting mix blended with sand and gravel. Regular potting mix holds too much moisture. In hot, sunny locales, give plants afternoon shade. Move nonhardy succulents indoors over winter in cold climates and keep them near a sunny window.

BHG TEST GARDEN TIP — MYRIAD CHOICES

Part of the fun in designing container gardens of succulents comes in choosing from the vast array of plant varieties and then planting them in a geometric pattern. Multiply echeverias and similar species by transferring their new little rosettes into small pots of sandy potting mix.

Sun Dance

Carefree succulents are naturals for containers. With their laid-back personalities, the plants thrive in toasty, well-drained environs. Succulents' fleshy, water-storing leaves earn them their catchall name as well as high praise for creating fascinating textures.

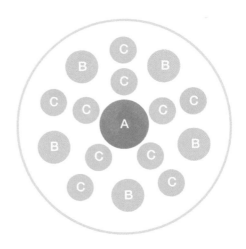

Creative Splash

Take advantage of hardy succulents' penchant for well-draining, sun-baked conditions and then transform a worn fountain (without a water supply) into a planter for them. From spring through fall, the fountain will once again overflow with life.

Essentials

Container: Two-tier concrete fountain
Light: Sun
Water: Allow soil to dry between waterings.

Ingredients

Top bowl:

A. 4 stringy stonecrop (*Sedum sarmentosum*)

Bottom bowl:

A. 4 stringy stonecrop (*Sedum sarmentosum*)

B. 4 two-row stonecrop (*Sedum spurium* 'John Creech')

Notes

Before planting, cover the bottom of each bowl with pea gravel to enhance drainage. Both sedum varieties creep and trail by nature, spreading via their shallow roots and filling the planters within a season. They'll gradually "trickle" over the planters' edges.

ALTERNATIVE PLANTINGS

Mature succulents will flower, but the plants are typically most valued for their foliage. If you want flowers, plant moss rose (*Portulaca*), a drought-tolerant annual, in your fountain.

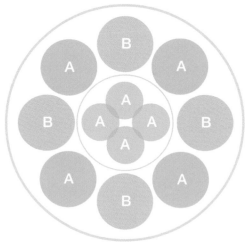

Essentials

Container: 12×22-inch earthenware jar

Light: Sun

Water: When soil feels dry

Ingredients

A. 1 fountain grass ('Hameln')

B. 4 Mexican feather grass (*Nassella tenuissima* 'Ponytails')

Notes

Ornamental grasses need no more than a dose of a slow-release fertilizer worked into the potting mix at planting time to see them through the growing season.

HALE AND HARDY

TEST GARDEN TIP

Like other long-term plants, ornamental grasses lose zones of hardiness when they spend the winter in a container. Fountain grass and feather grass, which are ordinarily hardy to Zone 4, should be able to survive the winter in a pot in Zone 6. Otherwise, transfer the plants to your in-ground garden in early fall.

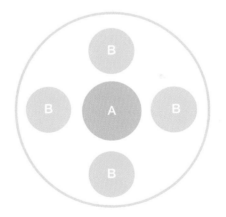

Leaves of Grass

Ornamental grasses blend subtle colors with airy textures in all-season displays. They outperform flowers by creating poetry in motion with their dancing forms and rustling sounds. For best results, combine an upright grass with an arching variety. Choose grasses with similar requirements for light and water.

Lovely & Lemony

Lemongrass, a tropical herb hardy to Zone 9, flourishes throughout the growing season in a container and then gives you a bonus: a harvest of edible stalks, popular in many types of Asian and Caribbean cooking.

Essentials

Container: 20-inch synthetic urn

Light: Sun

Water: Keep soil damp.

Ingredients

A. 1 lemongrass

B. 1 bacopa ('Snowstorm Pink')

C. 1 heuchera ('Dolce Mocha Mint')

D. 1 gooseneck loosestrife (*Lysimachia clethroides* 'Snow Candle')

Notes

Harvest perennial lemongrass in late summer or early fall and use it in cooking or for making tea. Start next year's crop by saving a stalk or two with roots attached; cut off the greenest portion and replant the root end. Keep the plant indoors through the winter.

ALTERNATIVE PLANTINGS

Replace the lemongrass with another perennial grass that will take beautifully to container life, such as feather reed grass (*Calamagrostis*), fescue (*Festuca*), porcupinegrass (*Miscanthus*), or switch grass (*Panicum*).

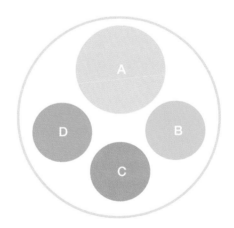

Essentials

Container: 20-inch stone-look urn

Light: Sun

Water: When soil begins to feel dry

Ingredients

(for each container)

A. 6 pale pink petunia (trailing type)

B. 4 licorice plant ('Splash')

C. 4 black-purple sweet potato

D. 1 pale pink geranium

E. 3 licorice plant ('Icicles')

Notes

Many newer petunia varieties don't require deadheading, but they will benefit from pinching occasionally and shearing by one-third in midseason. Monthly feeding helps keep petunias blooming all summer. Overwatering can cause plants to become leggy (with lots of stems and few flowers).

BLOOMING ON AND ON

Besides petunia, include any of these long-blooming annuals in your container gardens for nonstop flowers from spring into fall: dianthus, marigold, salvia, snapdragon, verbena, wax begonia, and zinnia.

Marathon Bloomers

A pair of large containers standing at eye level and flanking a front walk will wow passersby as well as visitors with a profusion of annuals that bloom continously throughout the growing season. Those who come close will be rewarded with the sweet scent of petunias.

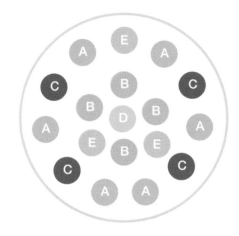

Leaps & Bounds

Compatibility with your home's architecture is key when placing a potted garden near a front door and wall. As planted, this vintage urn complements a Mediterranean-style home. It would suit many modern suburban landscapes, especially those with paved outdoor spaces and hot, dry conditions.

Essentials

Container: 20-inch cast-iron urn

Light: Part shade

Water: When the soil feels dry; pour water into the vaselike center of bromeliads.

Ingredients

A. 1 New Zealand flax (Rainbow hybrid)

B. 1 lotus vine

C. 1 bromeliad

D. 1 croton

Notes

This garden is a natural in Zones 9–11, where these plants live outdoors year-round, but it would be spectacular indoors too.

BHG CAN-DO DESIGN — RULE OF THIRDS

Let an accent or focal plant reach high and claim one-third of the design. Let one plant balance the effect as a low element while the supporting players fill out the design's other one-third.

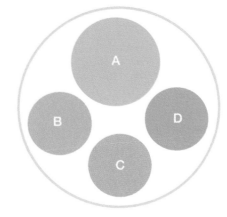

Essentials

Container: 24-inch glazed ceramic pot

Light: Part shade to sun

Water: When soil feels dry

Ingredients

A. 1 giant Burmese honeysuckle

B. 1 bacopa

C. 1 Santa Barbara daisy

D. 1 lilac vine (*Hardenbergia violacea* 'Happy Wanderer')

Notes

Growing a woody vine in a container garden requires a strong support. The trellis used in this scheme is anchored in the container and then to the house. The vines can take annual pruning to rein in their robust growth. Standing the container next to a porch pillar, balcony railing, or a fence gives less-vigorous vines a leg up.

BHG TEST GARDEN TIP

ALTERNATIVE PLANTINGS

Woody vines for colder climates include climbing hydrangea, porcelain berry (*Ampelopsis*), trumpet creeper (*Campsis radicans*), and wisteria.

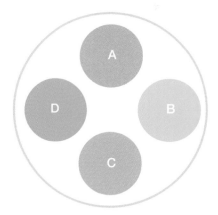

Rising Stars

This dramatic design has a practical side too: It softens the transition from an expanse of yard to the hard, upright surfaces of walls. The large, hefty pot holds a trellis for the climbing plants and enables the striking display, even in a small area.

What Goes Around

A dwarf conifer provides an evergreen framework for a potted scheme. Accompanying it with other long-season green plants produces a textural composition. For special occasions, you can dress up the greenery by tucking in a small vase of colorful cut flowers.

Essentials

Container: 12-inch wooden planter
Light: Part shade
Water: Keep soil damp.

Ingredients

A. 1 false cypress ('Ellwoodii')
B. 1 creeping thyme
C. 1 wintercreeper (*Euonymous* 'Gold Splash')

Notes

Bring the potted dwarf conifer indoors in fall and use it as a tabletop tree through the holiday season. Keep the plant in a cool room and the soil evenly damp before moving the container back outdoors in spring.

BHG container BASICS — USE A COASTER

Disguise a pot saucer or tray using preserved sheet moss. It will give your container garden a more natural appearance and help protect the surface of a tabletop at the same time.

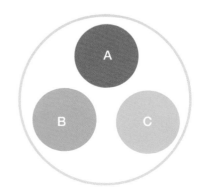

Essentials

Container: 14-inch glazed ceramic pot

Light: Part shade to shade

Water: Keep soil damp.

Ingredients

A. 1 button fern

B. 1 peacock plant *(Calathea)*

C. 1 pink geranium (Martha Washington)

D. 1 rex begonia

E. 1 pink cyclamen

Notes

Keep this potted garden going year-round. Between late summer and spring, place it indoors in a site where it will receive bright, indirect light. Before you let this potted garden vacation outdoors over the summer, remove the geranium from the container and transplant it into a separate pot to allow all the plants more growing room. Set the potted garden in a place where it will not receive direct sun. Place the geranium in a partly sunny spot.

BHG TEST GARDEN TIP · B REX

Rex begonias need high humidity and cool shade during the hot, dry days of summer. When growing a rex begonia on its own, set the potted plant on a large saucer or tray filled with wet gravel to boost humidity.

In the Pink

Look to houseplants for a wide selection of dramatically textured and colorful foliage. Group three or five plants with similar needs for light and water, then plant them together in a complementary pot that provides enough room for their growth.

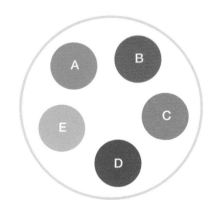

Keeping Romance Alive

Who can resist the allure of an instant garden, let alone one that conjures special effects? Plant this centerpiece in minutes using two colors of the same plant. You'll appreciate its long-lasting beauty as well as the source of glowing candlelight on an outdoor table.

Essentials

Container: 12×12×6-inch flexible stone-veneer planter

Materials: Glass hurricane globe; taper candle

Light: Part shade to shade

Water: When soil begins to feel dry

Ingredients

A. 2 heuchera ('Dolce Mocha Mint')

B. 2 heuchera ('Dolce Key Lime Pie')

Notes

Choose from a new generation of heuchera—coral bells—with bold-color foliage, vigorous adaptability, and delicious-sounding names for strong additions to long-lasting container gardens. You'll find options with leaf colors including chartreuse, amber, orange, purple, and black.

BHG TEST GARDEN TIP — SUPERIOR PERENNIAL

Move the heuchera to the garden at the end of summer. The plants will adapt quickly to garden beds where they get heat and sun, but they will fare best in part shade and cool weather.

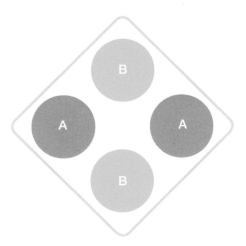

Essentials

Container: 18-inch glazed frostproof pot

Light: Part shade to shade

Water: Keep soil damp.

Ingredients

A. 1 blue lacecap hydrangea

B. 2 English ivy

C. 2 leatherleaf fern

D. 2 purple viola

E. 1 chartreuse licorice plant

Notes

Tuck bright green reindeer moss (from a crafts store) in between the young plants to heighten the contrast between them and enhance the garden's overall appeal. As the plants mature, they'll gradually hide the moss.

BHG TEST GARDEN TIP

POT ON
A hydrangea or other shrub will outgrow its container every two to three years. In early spring, before the plant resumes growth, transplant it into a larger pot to promote growth and flowering. Repot the shrub using fresh potting mix and water it thoroughly after transplanting.

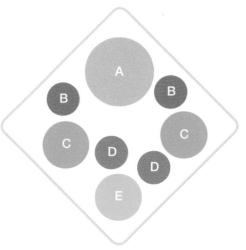

Blue Heaven

Launch the gardening season with this gorgeous scheme. Depending on where you live, start it indoors in late winter or early spring and then move it outdoors once warm weather has come to stay. In late summer transplant the hydrangea into the garden. Save the ferns for next year's container.

All Dressed Up

Centering your potted garden design on a long-term focal point, such as a dwarf arborvitae, will take it from one season into the next for at least two years. Change the annual underplantings for spring-to-fall and fall-to-spring displays.

Essentials

Container: 18-inch polystyrene planter

Light: Shade

Water: Keep soil damp.

Ingredients

A. 1 arborvitae

B. 6 pink impatiens

C. 4 blue-purple wishbone flower (*Torenia*)

D. 3 variegated trailing vinca ('Wojo's Jem')

Notes

Consider a polystyrene (foam) container for your next long-term potted garden. The lightweight, nonporous material will make the garden more portable, less thirsty for water, and less susceptible to temperature extremes.

BHG CAN-DO DESIGN

LEADERSHIP ROLE
It isn't necessary to place the focal-point plant in the center of a potted garden. Think about where the container will be displayed, how it will be viewed, and how the plants will best balance one another. Then plant accordingly.

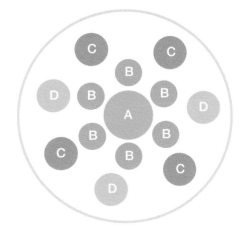

Essentials

Container: 36-inch steel window box frame with copper liner

Light: Shade

Water: Keep soil damp.

Ingredients

A. 4 impatiens

B. 2 Jacob's ladder ('Brise d'Anjou')

C. 2 hosta

D. 2 variegated ground ivy

E. 2 purple plectranthus

F. 1 sweet potato

G. 3 upright fuchsia

Notes

Choose a window box that's at least 8 inches deep to give plant roots room to grow and to save you from watering more than once a day during hot weather.

BHG container BASICS · PROPER MOUNTING

Prevent future problems and damage to your house by properly mounting a window box. Using sturdy brackets or lag bolts (and lead anchors in a brick house), secure the box to the wall rather than the window trim.

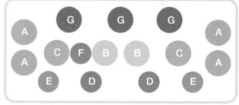

Facing Northside

Visible from indoors, a bright and colorful container brings cheer to the shady side of a house. The copper box and steel frame are made to last and sized to fit a standard window frame.

Welcoming Committee

Terra-cotta pots are the perfect color accompaniment to fall plantings. Let them be the centerpiece of your autumn decorations in this welcoming tower of seasonal plants and colors.

Essentials

Container: 12-inch terra-cotta pot; 24-inch lightweight terra-cotta-look pot

Light: Part shade

Water: Keep soil damp.

Ingredients

Top pot

A. 1 yellow-leaf hosta ('Stained Glass')

B. 1 red fountain grass ('Rubrum')

C. 2 kale ('Nagoya Rose')

D. 1 moneywort ('Aurea')

E. 1 red-leaf sedum ('Sunset Cloud')

Bottom pot

E. 1 red-leaf sedum ('Sunset Cloud')

F. 2 pink daisy mum

G. 1 orange sedge

H. 1 Swiss chard ('Bright Lights')

I. 2 pink-and-yellow snapdragon

J. 2 moneywort ('Golden Globe')

K. 1 heuchera ('Palace Purple')

L. 2 pansy ('Icicle')

M. 2 orange mum ('Ashley')

Notes

To make this tower, simply snuggle a long tom or a tall standard pot into the soil of a larger, broader container. Help secure it by pushing a bamboo garden stake through the top pot's drain hole into the larger pot below it. Add plants and you're ready to step back and enjoy the season-extending show.

Essentials

Container: 14-inch-square galvanized box

Light: Sun

Water: Keep soil damp.

Ingredients

A. 4 variegated sedge ('Evergold')

B. 2 aster ('Purple Dome')

C. 1 ornamental kale ('Nagoya')

Notes

Many colorful annuals thrive in cool fall weather and even shake off frost. Use these generously in your autumn containers: marguerite daisy, ornamental cabbage, twinspur (*Diascia* hybrids), dusty miller, African daisy, pansy, sweet alyssum, snapdragon, stock *(Matthiola incana)*, and chrysanthemum.

BHG container BASICS · INSTANT IMPACT

Instantly achieve pleasing results by filling a container with mature plants. Large, fully blooming plants look well established. The most colorful ones provide maximum decorative effect. When shopping, avoid annuals that have reached their peak and will soon set seed and fade.

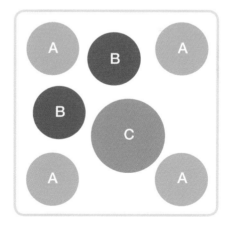

Fall Fireworks

Visit a local garden center in late summer or early fall to round up some cool-season plants. Tuck a few brightly colored selections into an unusual container just for fun or freshen existing displays by replacing tired-looking summer annuals with fall bloomers.

Autumn Attractions

Bring the warm hues of a harvest-season sunset to linger on your windowsill. Allow for seasonal changes in a window box by fitting it with a plastic liner at planting time.

Essentials

Container: 36-inch window box with 35-inch plastic liner

Light: Part shade to sun

Water: Keep soil damp.

Ingredients

A. 3 asparagus fern

B. 2 chrysanthemum ('Copper Charm')

C. 2 euphorbia ('Diamond Frost')

D. 1 hydrangea ('Alpenglow')

E. 2 sedge ('Toffee Twist')

F. 2 sweet william ('Amazon Rose Magic')

Notes

The planter's vintage-look patina comes with a coat of crackling glaze followed by a top coat of milk paint.

BHG container BASICS CHANGING PLACES

When chilly weather arrives, move the ferns indoors for the winter. Transplant the other plants into the garden.

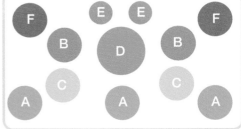

Essentials

Container: Two 15-inch terra-cotta pots

Light: Part shade

Water: When the soil feels dry

Ingredients

Pot 1

A. 1 eastern hemlock

B. 1 heuchera ('Dolce Crème Brûlée')

C. 1 moneywort ('Aurea')

Pot 2

D. 1 sedum ('Angelina')

E. 1 blue fescue ('Elijah Blue')

F. 1 oregano ('Kent Beauty')

G. 1 juniper ('Holger')

Notes

Cold-hardy perennials rally round young conifers, enlivening the dragonscale planters continuously for a year or two in mild regions. Unless frostproof, in frigid climates your pots should be emptied and stored for the winter and the plants given permanent places in the garden.

 LABELS ARE TELLING

If the plant label doesn't specify a range of hardiness zones, you cannot be sure of the plant's viability in your region. Think twice about the purchase, unless you know the plant or intend to grow it as an annual.

Home Sweet Home

These low-maintenance gardens feature easy-care plants with moderate growth rates, few pest or disease problems, and little upkeep besides watering. The all-foliage compositions boast bright hues and contrasting textures.

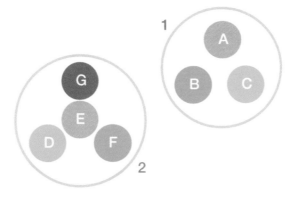

Evergreen Grace

Guided by a stout stake, a topiary's artful form takes advantage of the tree's naturally pendent branchlets. The evergreen's companions highlight and echo it with silvery and blue-gray foliage. The container makes its own strong statement.

Essentials

Container: 22-inch fiberglass planter

Light: Part shade

Water: When soil begins to feel dry

Ingredients

A. 1 weeping blue atlas cedar ('Glauca Pendula')

B. 3 kale

C. 2 licorice plant

D. 2 blue flax

E. 1 blue fescue ('Elijah Blue')

F. 1 dusty miller

Notes

When a tree has been trained to exhibit an unusual form, it will likely come from the nursery attached to a sturdy stake. Leave the tree secured to this stake when transplanting the works into a new container. If the stake is flimsy, carefully replace it and secure the tree to a new support using soft ties.

BHG container BASICS · YEAR IN, YEAR OUT

When you're looking for plants that will live contentedly in a container year-round, include a slow-growing tree or shrub. Possibilities include dwarf (meaning slow-growing or smaller than full-size species when mature) cultivars of evergreens, such as balsam fir, false cypress, juniper, mugo pine, and spruce.

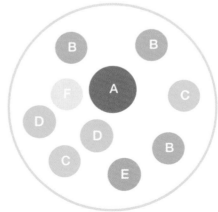

Essentials

Container: 36×11×9-inch cedar window box

Light: Part shade

Water: Apply warm water when the top inch of soil feels dry.

Ingredients

A. 1 dwarf cedar ('Port Orford')

B. 1 white cedar ('Sunkist')

C. 2 wintercreeper (*Euonymous* 'Emerald Gaiety')

D. 1 winter heather

E. 1 white cedar ('Rheingold')

F. 1 false cypress ('Boulevard')

G. 1 false cypress ('Elwoodii')

H. 1 false cypress ('Hinoki')

Notes

A layer of mulch slows moisture loss on sunny days. Spray an antidessicant (from a garden center) on evergreens, following product directions, to help prevent damage from winter winds.

READY FOR THE COLD
Make sure the dwarf conifers and other evergreens you select for your planter are winter-hardy in your area. Move the planter to a protected place if necessary.

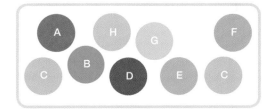

Winter Wonderland

Finish the gardening season by filling a generously deep window box with festive elfin shrubs, then enjoy a cheery evergreen landscape right outside your window through the fall and winter.

CHAPTER FOUR

Decorating
with Containers

Amp up the color on porches, patios, terraces—and even in the landscape—with containers. From small to large, containers add instant decor.

107

113

125

Easy Does It

When you take a simplified approach to creating container gardens, chances are you'll enjoy the process more without feeling overwhelmed or underfunded. The easiest schemes typically include a restrained plant selection. Many of the designs shown on the pages ahead are quick to make yet sure to attain maximum impact, using easy-care plants with long-lasting flowers or showy foliage.

Some of the most efficient container gardens fulfill more than one purpose: The plants are decorative and edible, or they combine a water feature with plantings, for instance. Your container garden might function as garden art, outdoor lighting, or long-term landscaping.

Sustainable gardens include plants, such as perennials or shrubs, that can live for several years in containers, needing minimal maintenance and resources. They may feature native plants, provide a food source or habitat for wildlife, or live in harmony with nature throughout the seasons. Your sustainable garden's health relies on organic gardening techniques with positive environmental consequences.

Go for the drama

Creating instant, entertaining, or surprising effects with containers depends on your planting choices. Whether large or small, dramatic or subtle, some plants are too wonderful to be appreciated anywhere but as stars in potted habitats.

Containers often provide ideal homes for special plants that benefit from nurturing before settling into larger garden life. The container itself makes an artful statement, while the planting provides a finishing touch.

The most special containers often have qualities and effects beyond our conception. The wonders of water—especially moving water—and plants combined in a pot never cease to intrigue. Arranged like cut flowers for special occasions, some potted displays decorate a tabletop or accent an entry in a way that greets guests and makes them feel welcome. Some containers entertain with their novelty; others boost spirits with their enduring appeal.

opposite Dynamic combinations of purple and yellow annuals, including zinnia, verbena, heliotrope, and Persian shield, add bold color to a patio. **above** Decorate a tabletop in a flash with identical plantings of young ornamental grasses, such as annual 'Pink Crystals' ruby grass (*Melinus nerviglumis*). Pop them into simple terra-cotta pots, balance them on stone bases, and top with attractive mulch. Easy and oh-so-simple. **below** Group containers and natural elements such as river stones to add high style to ho-hum corners.

Potted Water Gardens

A water garden offers more benefits than meet the eye. First, it introduces to you and visitors a world of fascinating water-loving plants not ordinarily found in container gardens. Add the gentle, soothing sound of trickling water to a potted garden and you'll multiply the pleasures it brings in other ways: The sound creates a relaxing ambience, masks obtrusive noise such as nearby traffic, and entices birds to take a dip or a drink.

Whether using a potted water garden as a year-round asset in a mild climate or for temporary beauty in a colder region, anyone can appreciate the minimal expense and maintenance involved. Set up your potted water garden and start reaping the rewards in a single afternoon.

Do it yourself

Any container will work as long as it is watertight and at least 6 inches deep. A 12-inch bowl holds potential for delight, especially when situated on a tabletop. A larger, deeper container can host a wider variety of plants along with a fountain while serving as a striking feature in the landscape.

Place your potted water garden where you'll enjoy it the most. Consider raising it above ground level or using a tall container to make it easily seen and heard. Keep the container within reach of a hose so you can replenish its water regularly.

Situate water-loving plants at their preferred depth with roots submerged or crowns (growing points) floating on the water's surface. Plant tags should help you determine the best growing conditions for your plants. Start with only two or three plants if the container's diameter is 18 inches or less. Feature a single type of plant or a variety in a larger container to achieve different effects.

left Large concrete containers of cattails catch water from a wall fountain. The patterned planting would be effective even without the fountain element. **above** A large, sturdy glazed pot becomes a stunning water feature and home to a lotus. **below** If you live in a cold-winter climate, treat water lettuce, dwarf umbrella plant, elephant's ear 'Black Magic', and other plants as annuals. Empty, clean, and store the pot before freezing weather arrives.

Anywhere Gardens

Your wish becomes a container garden's command when you have a spot and a purpose in mind for it. Starting at ground level, use containers' versatility to achieve various landscaping goals. Set them up, for example, to edge a pathway, screen a sitting area, or frame an entry. Containers' portability enables you to stage them where they will put on the best show or move them elsewhere if need be.

When you look for places to stage containers, consider sites without in-ground growing room. Potted gardens turn decks, patios, and other outdoor spaces into alluring destinations, integrating them with the landscape. Whatever the size of your outdoor area, potted plants provide instant color, form, and interest. Depending on where you place them, containers complement structures and balance hardscape elements.

Use a single pot to showcase a favorite plant, giving it center stage in a bed, or to fill a gap in the garden where a plant has failed or passed its prime. Mixing plants in a large pot or grouping multiple pots helps paint a garden picture. But the key is not how many pots you have; it's what you do with them.

Make a first impression

Positioning containers at your front door highlights the entry, providing a pleasing first impression. Edging a path with pots guides visitors' steps. On stairs, pots bring attention to changes in level and accentuate the architecture. Pots can also define the perimeter of a garden, paved area, or similar landscape element while softening the hard surface. A big-enough potted garden disguises an unsightly view.

Deliberately setting pots here and there can create a sense of movement. Where there's a practical reason for lining up containers—along the perimeter of an outdoor room to boost privacy, for instance—repetition fulfills the task.

opposite A chorus line of potted Madagascar dragontree *(Dracaena marginata)* works well to screen an intimate dining area without blocking the fantastic view. **below left** Survey your site, then match potted gardens to opportunities. Several pots of lavender, pansies, and petunias step up to colorfully mark an entryway. **below right** Pots of red dragon wing begonias provide portable spots of color wherever they are most needed from spring into fall.

Raising Your Sights

Take your container gardens to the next level, literally, by raising them off the ground. Elevating a container—anywhere between the ground and eye level—makes it easier to see and appreciate its contents from a distance or within sniffing range. Propped on a plant stand, ledge, wall, or windowsill, a potted garden becomes a showpiece, decorative enough to boost your home's curb appeal. And there's a bonus: When you create plantable areas at more accessible levels, you can garden without crouching or bending—a boon to your back and knees.

Grow vertically

Using the vertical dimension helps you make the most of every inch of potential gardening space and make room to garden where there doesn't seem to be any. Window boxes in particular serve many apartment dwellers as the only option for gardening. Where there's a wall, fence, or railing, opportunity exists to parlay available surfaces into space for planting that also makes the structure more appealing.

Take time to explore the array of containers made especially for decks, porches, balconies, and windowsills. Window boxes and lined metal baskets can also be secured to other locations such as porch or deck railings. Use wide, deep planters whenever possible to cover more area with plants. Experiment with cascading plants, including flowering (ivy geraniums and petunias) as well as foliage-only (trailing vinca and plectranthus) options.

The size of usable containers may be limited by their weight when mounted on walls, fences, and railings. Although a steel hayrack lined with coco fiber and filled with ultralight potting mix proves lighter than a large cedar window box, the weight of both increases considerably when saturated with water. Use high-quality containers and building materials; plan to mount containers without taking shortcuts or damaging any structures involved.

opposite A tiered plant stand offers an easy way to decorate a wall with the seasonal color of pansies and forget-me-nots. **above** If space is limited, look for ways to grow vertically using cascading plants, such as sweet potato, moneywort, spiderwort, and trailing vinca. **below** For best results, hang window boxes that are slightly wider than the window frame. Fill them with long-blooming plants such as petunias and fan flower.

Aiming Higher

When planning container gardens, remember to look up! Container gardens raised to eye level or higher instantly garner attention. When you place favorite plants on a pedestal or choreograph a combination in a high flowering basket, you'll improve the setting and possibly heighten your gardening skills too.

Plant aerial gardens

Imagine where you might create special interest with a potted garden on a pedestal. An urn serves as a pot with a built-in pedestal. But you can easily fashion a support for almost any pot using a sturdy base such as a concrete block or an overturned pot.

You'll find a new generation of containers similar to hanging baskets but made for mounting on railings, posts, or poles. Freestanding towers with tiered baskets or trellises support trailing plants and provide height anywhere they're needed.

Make the most of hanging plantings (unless they're designed for a wall or fence) by looking for a way to ensure they're visible from all sides. In exchange for the impression made by hanging baskets' voluptuousness, extra maintenance will be needed. The plants in aerial containers often require more watering and feeding because their roots are particularly confined and subject to the drying effects of air circulation. Hang them within reach for convenient watering. Take extra steps to secure any suspended containers. Plenty of sturdy hooks, brackets, and other supports are available to help you handle the job.

On the plus side, aerial containers give you opportunities to incorporate types of plants that expand the use of vertical space. Plants that climb, trail, and cascade are natural acrobats that will enhance your displays. Arrays of petunias, verbenas, ivies, and others are popular for their abilities to tumble and camouflage a hanging basket. Your choice of plants and planting methods can ensure that the container packs a strong visual punch.

left Fast-growing sweet potato vines spilling out of hanging baskets create a lively privacy screen. **above** Massive moss-lined baskets, packed with impatiens and other shade-loving plants, provide color around a gazebo with little upkeep. **below** A freestanding container overflowing with Wave petunias, strawflowers, and creeping zinnias adds three-dimensional color to a garden.

Special Strategies

You don't need a magic wand to become a garden magician. Potted gardens help you expand the potential of any area when you apply visual tricks. Strategically placing containers can lead the eye or distract it, creating an illusion of depth, height, and overall space.

Containers also help you put your gardenable space to good use. You'll gain floor space anytime you raise containers off the ground and use vertical areas to display plantings instead. Wall planters and other hanging containers make it possible to garden in the narrowest spaces (between a house and a fence or between apartment buildings). In addition, you'll minimize the blankness of a wall or fence with containers placed on or near the structure.

Any hanging garden or vertical planting draws the eye upward and extends the feeling of space. On a balcony or porch, for instance, a staged potted garden partially conceals the view and emphasizes a sense of the beyond. Similarly, situating a container on a far wall or in the farthest corner of a patio creates an illusion of depth and increased distance. Employing containers to partition an area into outdoor rooms also gives an impression of size. One way or the other, containers transform a tiny, confined, dull, or otherwise limited space into a lush, interesting garden.

Stage for effect

A deck or patio presents an opportunity for a plant stand, shelving, or similar platform for staging potted plants in space-saving tiers. Combining cool-color plants (especially blues and purples) and pastels strengthens an illusion of depth.

A solitary container enables you to plant a miniature landscape—including a small tree or shrub and colorful underplantings—even in the smallest of spaces. Another way to add height to any container entails outfitting it with a trellis and a climbing plant.

opposite Cedar window boxes and bright tuberous begonias turn an expanse of gray fence into a wall of blooms. **below left** Large concrete bowls planted with turfgrass add lawnlike greenery to a small patio. Occasional trimming keeps the grass under control. **below right** Placed at various heights, potted gardens flank a path with wax begonias, coleus, and other shade plants.

Decking Out Porches

Container plantings are one of the simplest ways to dress up porches. In addition to making your home look more attractive and welcoming, a container-laden front porch also improves the view from inside the house. The view of flower and foliage on plant stands, hanging from overhangs, and sitting on porch railings will be a vista you enjoy all summer.

Strategize for color

Every porch features a doorway into the house, so flanking this entrance is an obvious place to add containers. The symmetry of pots on either side of the door is so classic—and so easy to do. Get two large matching containers and plant them up. Doorways under porches are usually shaded, so choose shade-loving plants such as ivy, begonias, coleus, and ferns.

Styling steps with containers makes an attractive entryway. And this is your chance to amp up the color. If the steps leading to the porch receive ample sunlight, you can fill the containers with bright, sun-loving annuals such as geraniums, petunias, calibrachoa, fanflower, and sweet potato vine.

Adorning the railings is another way to add color to a porch. Rail planters come in a wide range of sizes and styles—in wood, resin, fiberglass, and metal. They can rest on top of the railing, be attached by brackets mounted on railings, or straddle the railing. Railing containers are heavy (especially after being watered). Make sure the railing is strong enough to handle the weight.

Hanging baskets add spots of overhead color on porches. You can also create a privacy screen by hanging baskets at various heights to create a wall of flowers and foliage. Hanging baskets require more water than other containers because they are exposed to more wind. Keep plants healthy by not allowing them to dry out.

opposite Flank a porch doorway with the a pair of planters for a simple, yet classic way to flower up an entryway. Here white urns hold overflowing begonias. **above right** Add container color to porches at all levels: on the floor, raised on pedestal plant stands and railing planters, and hanging from above. Here hanging lattice panels create privacy and are dressed up with attached containers filled with flowers and foliage plants. **right** Hanging planters, suspended at different heights, can create privacy. Containers made from repurposed funnels add a bit of whimsy to the view.

Containers in the Landscape

Container gardens can play functional as well as pretty roles in landscaping your yard. They don't have to be relegated to just decorating porches, patios, decks, and terraces. They also make excellent participants in front, back, and side yards.

Large containers add instant structure to a yard through strategic (yet simple!) placement. In the center of a lawn, a container becomes a focal point. Lay a path to it and the container becomes a destination. Add a pair of large containers at the edge of a patio and they become an entrance point to the yard.

Grow plants outside your zone

Containers also allow you to grow species of plants in your yard that you might not be able to grow in the ground. For example, you can add tropical flair or desert design (think large-leafy bananas or spiky agaves) to your yard when you plant them in containers. You can also grow plants where they can't grow in the ground, such as areas under shallow-rooted trees. Enjoy containers of shade-loving annuals such as hostas and begonias above the ground.

In garden beds, containers offer height. Choose a large container to serve as the centerpiece of a formal bed. Planted with trees or standard roses, a container can offer a gorgeous structural centerpiece. Likewise, container plantings can be sunk into the ground; for example, invasive plants such as mint can be corralled safely in a container planted directly into the ground.

Containers can take the place of in-ground plantings to create a neat and modern look. Try lining up matching pots planted with small trees or ornamental grasses in the side yard of your home.

opposite Raise the stakes in garden design by adding containers to the landscape on posts in the garden. An annual-packed container, with dusty miller, melampodium, angelonia, sweet potato vine, fanflower, and calibrachoa seems to hover in the garden. **below left** A small strip of ground alongside a house gets the topiary treatment with neatly coiffed pots of boxwood. **below right** A squat, ribbed pot holds court as the centerpiece of a circular garden. New Guinea impatiens bubble out of the top.

Sprucing Up Steps

Step up entryway and path decor with flower-filled containers. Stair steps provide ideal staging for pots and flowers, which can add instant impact to lackluster concrete or wooden stairs. A few well-placed containers can transform a functional set of rising steps into a beautiful stairway garden.

Placement is easy. If the steps are wide enough, stair-step containers from top to bottom, adding one pot per step. Use the same flowers and containers (simple terra-cotta works!). The repetition of identical pots and flowers, rising with uniformity up the stairs, draws the eye upward (or downward). What a beautiful way to welcome guests to your home.

Step up the color

Landings are another opportunity for container decor. Cluster a couple of containers to make an impromptu garden. For stairways built into the ground, you can set pots on the sides, making the passageway feel larger, more colorful, and grander.

Stairway container gardens have a flow of passersby, so it's a great place to add scented plants. Fragrant herbs such as lavender, rosemary, and thyme offer pleasing scents, especially it they are close enough to reach out and touch.

When placing containers on stairs, consider safety first. Pot placement should not impede traffic. Avoid clustering containers if that would make stepping difficult; the walkway should be wide and clear. Make sure pots are well positioned so that they don't create a stumbling hazard. They shouldn't be easy to dislodge (causing them to take a tumble).

If the stepping area of the stairs is too narrow for containers, use the railing space to perch pots. They can be attached below the handrail. If the stairway is enclosed, use the outer wall for container placement.

left Staircases offer perfect perches for a potted garden. A group of identical urns planted with purple petunias makes a colorful entryway to a front porch. **above** An out-of-use staircase offers the perfect staging for a bevy of containers. **below** Banded pot holders position flower-filled terra-cotta pots on the outside wall of a staircase. If stairs are too narrow, position containers on the outside of the staircase. Choose trailing varieties such as ivy and million bells to create a lovely curtain of foliage and flowers.

Combining Containers

Think of the adage "strength in numbers." While one container sitting alone on a porch or patio looks lonely, a crowd of containers looks festive and social. Because containers are so easy to plant and most, except for really large pots, are also easy to transport, it takes just a quick afternoon of potting to yield a cluster of colorful containers. A grouping of pots is a great way to create a focal point on a deck or patio or infuse bright color into a dark corner. And there are lots of creative ways to combine containers to achieve the outdoor decor look you want.

Cluster containers

If you want to create a contemporary look, line up same-size containers. Combine odd numbers—groups of three, five, and seven—to create the best look. Clusters of containers can be used to create outdoor room dividers: Line up a group of square planters to separate a seating area from a dining area.

You can also use a lineup of containers to create privacy screening. Use large containers planted with columnar-shape trees to build a living screen. Tall narrow shrub or tree choices include arborvitae, boxwood, and barberry.

A grouping of small-to-tall containers creates an oasis of color on decks or porches. Choose identical containers in different sizes; create a grouping of three containers using a small, medium, and large version. Many container manufacturers produce pots in multiple sizes, so it's easy to have this look.

Add variety to your container grouping by choosing vessels made of the same material, such as terra-cotta, galvanized metal, or wood. They don't have to match precisely; the materials impose the unified look.

opposite Groups can be made with objects on hand. Here a vintage wagon makes a great venue for small pots of sedums and succulents that might otherwise be overlooked. **above right** Group with gusto. Combine large planters of trees and shrubs with all-flower pots for a layered and textural look. Mix and match tropicals (such as leafy bananas) with topiary ivies, roses, and hydrangea—each in its own pot. **right** Create a unified look by using containers made from the same materials. Galvanized aluminum pots, tanks, and buckets can be found at farm supply and home improvement stores.

Sustainable Schemes

If your goal includes saving time, effort, or money, then it pays to understand how to make potted gardens that span the seasons. Get to know the perennials, shrubs, and trees that can live for several years in containers without requiring replacement. Highlight a container garden with at least one long-lived plant, whether it is evergreen or deciduous, and you'll save yourself the work of completely redoing a container each spring.

Where the climate is conducive, marathon plants offer year-round impact. Where the climate proves challenging to the plants' survival in a pot, there are better options than treating these long-lived plants as annuals and tossing them on the compost pile once freezing weather arrives. Wherever you live, it's possible to practice plant conservation, using careful planning and storage techniques to overwinter plants.

Think outside the box

Extend the longevity of your container gardens by turning to a greater array of planting options beyond annuals. Take advantage of plants you might not ordinarily think of using in containers, such as self-sufficient ornamental grasses, color-rich conifers, and long-flowering shrubs. Then play upon their architectural aspects. A woody vine or tree-form standard adds instant verticality to a design. Houseplants and succulents add appreciable contrasts in leaf size, texture, and color.

Containers provide an excellent opportunity to experiment with plants and learn more about how they behave and what they need. Consider the plants' ultimate sizes when planting and make sure the chosen container won't be overwhelmed by a plant as it matures. Beware of vigorous and spreading plants that will rapidly outgrow containers, exhaust the soil, and demand repotting or replacing. In the end, your favorite plants will likely include some that ask little but give much and earn a place in your permanent garden.

left A vintage copper washtub hosts a shade garden, including Japanese maple, hosta, coleus, and tassel fern. **above** Incorporating a young tree (ginkgo), a perennial (lilyturf), and an annual (fan flower) in a container expands your plant repertoire. **below** 'Tiger Eyes' is a well-behaved staghorn sumac *(Rhus typhina)* with brilliant foliage and a compact form that's ideal for a container.

Keeping Up Appearances

Practice a few basic gardening techniques to keep long-term potted gardens looking their best and extend your enjoyment of them.

Choose a spacious, sturdy, and frost-free container to accommodate plants destined for long-term relationships.

Start with high-quality, compost-enriched potting mix. Top off the potting mix in a container periodically because watering erodes it. Replenish long-term plantings by replacing at least one-third of the loose potting mix with a fresh, compost-enriched blend.

Feed plants by adding a time-release fertilizer to the potting mix at planting time. Supplement with a dose of liquid fertilizer as needed during growth periods.

After planting, cover the soil with an inch of mulch and tuck in drip irrigation to ensure soil moisture.

Remove spent flowers and leaves; lightly prune plants as needed to maintain their overall appearance.

Get ready for winter

In cold climates, give planters shelter and extra protection to help them survive winter. Water plants occasionally throughout winter.

Potted water gardens require specific attention to water quality and winterization.

IN THE ZONE When selecting plants for your potted gardens, choose ones that will be container-hardy in your zone, meaning ones that are two zones hardier than the zone where you live (see zone map on page 235). If you live in Zone 5, for example, choose plants that are designated as hardy to Zone 3 to help ensure their survival in a container garden. If you're willing to experiment with plants, they might surprise you by flourishing in a protected location with a microclimate that equates to one zone warmer—on a sunny enclosed patio or next to the south side of the house, for instance.

opposite Small-leaved boxwood and rosemary can be clipped into simple, geometric shapes using hand pruners or small hedge shears. **above** Easy-care Scotch moss carpets the soil of a potted lemon tree and demonstrates the creative use of a groundcover.

CHAPTER FIVE

Plant Encyclopedia

Choose plants that excel in sun, shade, and in between. From small trees and shrubs to trailing and vining plants, you'll find a beautiful palette of plants to work with.

140   162   178

African Daisy
Arctotis selections

Zones: **2–11**
Type: **Annual**
Height: **1–2 feet tall**
Width: **1 foot wide**
Color: **Red, yellow, orange, pink, white**
Bloom Time: **Summer through fall**

African daisy has a bold, graphic look that's hard to find in more common daisies. Flowers are big, up to 4 inches across, often with interesting eyelike markings around the flower's center. This cool-season plant hails from South Africa. In areas where summers aren't hot, such as the northern regions of the United States and the Pacific Northwest, it will bloom constantly until frost. In warm-summer areas, it often takes a break during the peak of summer but reblooms in fall. Many types have silvery-green leaves that remain attractive when the plant isn't in bloom. It's usually grown as an annual but is a perennial in frostfree climates.

Varieties

1 'THE RAVERS HEARTS AND TARTS' AFRICAN DAISY
Arctotis 'The Ravers Hearts and Tarts' has gray-green foliage and orange-and-pink flowers. It grows 12 inches tall and 16 inches wide.

2 SUN BRELLA 'TAURUS'
Sun Brella 'Taurus' grows 8 to 14 inches tall and is ideal for hanging baskets and window boxes. It's easy care because it doesn't require deadheading. It's an excellent early spring or autumn container plant.

CONTAINER COMPANIONS

ANGELONIA
Heat-loving annuals such as angelonia are perfect for growing with African daisy so you can enjoy blooms even in hot weather.

DIANTHUS
Add another dimension to your plantings by combining African daisy with fragrant varieties of dianthus.

STOCK
In spring and fall, plant upright-growing stock with African daisy to create a contrast in plant shapes.

Agapanthus
Agapanthus selections

Zones: 7–11
Type: **Perennial**
Height: **4 feet tall**
Width: **3 feet wide**
Color: **Blue, violet, lavender, white**
Bloom Time: **Summer through fall**

Agapanthus is a landscape staple in warm-winter regions, and it's no wonder why. This easy-to-grow perennial produces colorful globes of blue or white trumpet-shape flowers in summer and fall. Its strappy evergreen leaves add texture to beds, borders, and containers. Agapanthus blooms best in a spot where it gets full sun and has moist, well-drained soil. Divide it every three to four years to keep clumps healthy and vigorous. If you live in a cool-winter area, you can overwinter agapanthus in containers by bringing the pots to a cool (around 40°F) spot and watering them only once a month or so. In spring, move the containers back outdoors after all danger of frost has passed. Potted agapanthus is said to bloom best when slightly root-bound.

Varieties

1 *AGAPANTHUS AFRICANUS*
Agapanthus africanus is a common type with blue flowers that bloom in late summer and early fall. It grows 3 feet tall and 2 feet wide. Zones 9–10

2 'SNOW STORM' AGAPANTHUS
Agapanthus 'Snow Storm' is a fast-growing, floriferous selection that produces clusters of pure white flowers in late spring and summer. It grows 30 inches tall and wide. Zones 8–10

TEST GARDEN TIP
After agapanthus blooms fade, don't cut back foliage. The leaves provide nourishment for flowers next year.

CONTAINER COMPANIONS

SOCIETY GARLIC
Society garlic looks a bit like a miniature agapanthus; try mixing the two for a subtle contrast.

KANGAROO PAW
The spiky stems of tall kangaroo paw tower over agapanthus' rounded globe flowers.

BIRD OF PARADISE
Easy-to-grow orange bird of paradise is a sure bet to grow with blue agapanthus.

TEST GARDEN TIP

Agave's varied shapes and colors make it ideal for succulent bowls.

Agave
Agave selections

Zones: **5–11**
Type: **Perennial**
Height: **1–15 feet tall**
Width: **1–10 feet wide**
Color: **Greenish-yellow flowers; bluish-green foliage**
Bloom Time: **Summer**

Among the most architectural plants, agave features bold succulent leaves that set the tone for wherever they're planted. They're incredibly heat- and drought-tolerant and most are long-lived. Many varieties bear sharp spines along leaf margins and at the leaf tip, which adds to their dramatic presentation. The bluish-green rosettes naturally spread by producing offsets at the base of the plant. Agave is an excellent choice for sunny, hot, dry areas, especially desert regions, with good drainage.

Varieties

1 *AGAVE AMERICANA* 'MARGINATA'
Agave americana 'Marginata' is also called century plant because it blooms infrequently. After the mother plant blooms, it dies, but offsets continue to grow. It is a large plant, reaching up to 6 feet tall. Zones 10–11

2 *AGAVE ATTENUATA*
Agave attenuata is a common landscape plant in warm, dry climates. This agave develops thick trunks topped with spike-free gray-green leaves. It grows 3–6 feet tall and wide. Zones 9–11

CONTAINER COMPANIONS

LAVENDER
Lavender's silvery foliage and airy flower spikes create a nice contrast to the bold foliage of agave.

YUCCA
Yucca and agave have the same growth requirements, and their plant forms look great together.

PENSTEMON
Add color to beds and borders with agaves by planting bright, drought-tolerant penstemons.

Ageratum
Ageratum houstonianum

Type: **Annual**
Height: **6–36 inches tall**
Width: **6–18 inches wide**
Color: **Blue, lavender, white, rose**
Bloom Time: **Summer through fall**

Ageratum is such a little workhorse that nearly every garden should have some. This annual is an easy-to-grow, old-fashioned favorite that produces a steady show of colorful powder-pufflike flowers from late spring through frost. It's also rarely bothered by pests, so you count on it to look good. Plus, it provides some of the truest blues you can find in flowers—a rare thing. Plant in spring after all danger of frost has passed. Plant in groups of a dozen or more for best show. Deadhead and fertilize regularly for best blooms.

Varieties

1 'AZURE PEARL'
Ageratum 'Azure Pearl' features powder blue, frilly flowers that form a mass of color. Plants grow about 12 inches tall. Flowers are clear, lovely blue.

2 'HAWAII WHITE'
Ageratum 'Hawaii White' grows 6–8 inches tall and produces white flowers.

TEST GARDEN TIP
Plant a frilly edge of the shorter varieties of ageratum at the front of containers or window boxes.

CONTAINER COMPANIONS

SALVIA
Ageratum is a great partner for blue salvia, which has flowers that color-coordinate perfectly.

DUSTY MILLER
A classic combo, silvery dusty miller foliage is a perfect accent to ageratum's fluffy blooms.

FRENCH MARIGOLD
Create a bold contrast against ageratum's blue flowers with easy-growing orange or yellow marigolds.

TEST GARDEN TIP

If you have a bright, sunny spot indoors, you can even keep angelonia flowering all winter.

Angelonia
Angelonia selections

Zones: **9–10**
Type: **Annual**
Height: **1–2 feet tall**
Width: **1–2 feet wide**
Color: **White, pink, purple**
Bloom Time: **Summer through fall**

Angelonia is also called summer snapdragon, and once you get a good look at it, you'll know why. It has salvia-like flower spires that stretch a foot or 2 tall, but they're studded with fascinating snapdragon-like flowers with beautiful colorations in purple, white, or pink. It's the perfect plant for adding bright color to hot, sunny spaces. This tough plant blooms all summer long with spirelike spikes of blooms. While all varieties are beautiful, keep an eye out for the sweetly scented selections.

Varieties

1 'ANGELMIST DARK PLUM'
'Angelonia Dark Plum' is one of the darkest selections; it bears deep purple flowers all summer and grows 2 feet tall.

2 'ANGELMIST LAVENDER'
'Angelmist Lavender' offers clear lavender-purple blooms on 2-foot-tall plants.

CONTAINER COMPANIONS

DUSTY MILLER
Dusty miller's silvery leaves make a great foil for dark purple angelonia varieties.

GERANIUM
Geranium's round flower heads make a knockout combination with upright angelonia.

NASTURTIUM
Nasturtiums like hot, dry locations too; use yellow- or orange-blooming types to create contrast.

Arborvitae
Thuja selections

Zones: **3–9**
Type: **Shrub**
Height: **8 feet tall**
Width: **2 feet wide**
Color: **Dark and light green, yellow, and blue foliage**
Bloom Time: **Foliage looks good all year.**

Arborvitae will flourish where no other evergreen does, spreading a lush screen of fanlike foliage that provides privacy and provides winter shelter for birds. For garden sculptors, arborvitae offers just the right texture and growth habit for topiaries. Many dwarf varieties are available as fillers and vertical accents for smaller gardens. Arborvitae prospers in deeply cultivated, moist, fertile soil in full sun. When the shrubs outgrow their containers, plant them in your yard.

Varieties

1 'GOLDEN TUFFET'
'Golden Tuffet' features golden-orange foliage. This slow-growing arborvitae grows in width rather than height. Zones 3–8

2 *THUJA OCCIDENTALIS* 'MR. BOWLING BALL', EASTERN ARBORVITAE
Thuja occidentalis 'Mr. Bowling Ball' is a dwarf, rounded shrub with rich green leaf color and dense foliage. It grows 24 to 32 inches tall and wide. Zones 3–8

TEST GARDEN TIP
Choose dwarf varieties of arborvitae to provide year-round appeal for containers and window boxes.

CONTAINER COMPANIONS

'RHEINGOLD' ARBORVITAE
'Rheingold' bears golden foliage, sometimes pink-tinted when young; it mixes well with other small arborvitae.

'BLUE STAR' JUNIPER
'Blue Star' stands out for its silvery color and dense, ground-hugging habit. Grows 16 inches tall.

DWARF ALBERTA SPRUCE
A favorite for its dense growth, small needles, and nearly perfect cone-shape habit, dwarf Alberta spruce is a great container companion.

Aster

Aster selections

Zones: **3–9**
Type: **Perennial**
Height: **1–5 feet tall**
Width: **1 foot wide**
Color: **Purple, lavender, blue, white**
Bloom Time: **Late summer through fall**

Asters get their name from the Latin word for "star," and their flowers are indeed the superstars of the fall garden. Some types of this native plant can grow up to 6 feet tall with flowers in white and pinks but also, perhaps most strikingly, in rich purples and showy lavenders. Not all asters are fall bloomers. Extend the season by growing some of the summer bloomers as well. Some are naturally compact; tall types that grow more than 2 feet tall benefit from staking or an early-season pinching or cutting back by about one-third in July to keep the plant more compact.

Varieties

1 *ASTER NOVAE-ANGLIAE 'ALMA POTSCHKE'*
Aster novae-angliae 'Alma Potschke' blooms from August to frost with red-violet daisies on a plant 4 feet tall. Zones 4–8

2 *ASTER NOVI-BELGII 'FELLOWSHIP'*
Aster novi-belgii 'Fellowship' has clear pink daisy flowers on plants that reach 3 feet tall. Zones 4–8

CONTAINER COMPANIONS

BOLTONIA
Snowbank boltonia looks like a larger version of aster. It is a closely related cousin. Its pure-white daisylike blooms team beautifully with pink or purple fall-blooming asters.

RUSSIAN SAGE
The lavender spires of Russian sage blooms create a nice contrast to the mounded plant form of asters. Color-coordinate with either purple or pink asters for a showstopping sunny late-summer border.

Bacopa
Sutera selections

Zones: 2–11
Type: **Annual**
Height: **4–8 inches tall**
Width: **2–3 feet wide**
Color: **White, light blue, pink, violet**
Bloom Time: **Summer through fall**

Bacopa was once an unusual flower, but it's become very popular in garden centers. And why not? It's adorable! This plant has long, cascading stems that smother themselves in tiny, perfect, five-petal flowers. It's become a favorite for selling in hanging baskets where its pretty trailing habit can be shown off. Also try in pots, planters, and window boxes. Unlike many plants, bacopa doesn't tend to wilt when it gets dried out. Instead, it loses its flowers and may take two or three weeks to begin blooming again. Keep it evenly watered for continuous bloom.

Varieties

1 'SNOWSTORM BLUE'
Sutera cordata 'Snowstorm Blue' shows off large lavender-blue flowers. It trails to 36 inches or more.

2 'SNOWSTORM'
Sutera cordata 'Snowstorm' offers small white flowers on 36-inch trailing plants.

TEST GARDEN TIP
Fertilize often during the summer for best results. Keep plants well-watered or flowers will drop.

CONTAINER COMPANIONS

BEGONIA
These upright beauties sometimes look a little naked at the base, and bacopa makes a great pot dressing.

GERANIUM
Take an ordinary geranium in a container from humdrum to wow with vigorous bacopa cascading over the rim.

PETUNIA
Bacopa's tiny flowers sparkle in contrast to big, blowsy petunias.

Black-Eyed Susan

Rudbeckia selections

Zones: **2–11**
Type: **Annual, perennial**
Height: **2–10 feet tall**
Width: **1½–3 feet wide**
Color: **Yellow, orange**
Bloom Time: **Midsummer through fall**

Add a pool of sunshine to the garden with a massed planting of black-eyed Susan. From midsummer, these tough native plants bloom their golden heads off in sun or light shade and mix well with other perennials, annuals, and shrubs. Tall varieties look especially appropriate among shrubs, which in turn provide support. Add black-eyed Susan to wildflower meadows or native plant gardens for a naturalized look. Average soil is sufficient for black-eyed Susan, but it should be able to hold moisture fairly well.

Varieties

1 'AUTUMN COLORS'
Rudbeckia 'Autumn Colors' is an award-winning annual series that bears 5-inch-wide gold flowers flushed with bronze, red, and rust. It grows 2 feet tall.

2 BROWN-EYED SUSAN
Rudbeckia triloba is a North American native biennial or short-lived perennial that has clusters of small yellow flowers in summer and autumn. It grows 5 feet tall and 3 feet wide. Zones 4–7

CONTAINER COMPANIONS

FOUNTAIN GRASS
With slender arching grassy leaves and bottlebrush panicles of flower spikelets, fountain grass brings a rustic grace to massed plantings of 'Goldsturm' black-eyed Susan. They enjoy similar conditions.

RUSSIAN SAGE
In sunny gardens, the wandlike flower stems of lavender Russian sage play well against black-eyed Susan.

Boxwood
Buxus selections

Zones: **5–8**
Type: **Perennial, shrub**
Height: **15 feet tall**
Width: **15 feet wide**
Color: **White; blue-green or variegated leaves; white flowers**
Bloom Time: **Spring**

An evergreen shrub ideal for sculpting, boxwood can take the shape of a neat mound or grow into small green clouds of foliage if left unmanicured. It's one of the most popular choices for garden topiaries. This fragrant shrub is frequently used as an outliner and definer around garden beds and paths even when planted in containers. Garden neat freaks will want to wield the pruning shears frequently to keep boxwood in bounds. Provide a well-drained soil mix for boxwood to prevent problems with root rot.

Varieties

1 'GREEN GEM'
Buxus 'Green Gem' is a compact variety with dark green leaves that retain their color well in cold winters. It grows only 2 feet tall and wide. Zones 4–8

2 'GREENMOUND'
Buxus 'Greenmound' retains its bright green color through the darkest winter days. It's compact (to 3 feet tall and 4 feet wide), slow growing, and extra cold hardy. Zones 4–8

TEST GARDEN TIP
Boxwoods clipped to a particular shape need frequent snipping to retain their form.

CONTAINER COMPANIONS

CATMINT
Combine loose mounds of gray-green catmint with tightly clipped boxwood for a beautiful contrast in large containers. The blue catmint flowers contrast nicely with boxwood's emerald green foliage.

CREEPING HERBS
Plant creeping varieties of herbs, such as prostrate rosemary and creeping thyme, with small boxwood plants.

Butterfly Bush
Buddleja selections

Zones: **5–10**
Type: **Shrub**
Height: **3–4 feet tall**
Width: **Up to 3 feet wide**
Color: **White, pink, blue, violet, red, yellow; gray/silver or variegated leaves**
Bloom Time: **Summer through fall**

Drenching the air with a fruity scent, butterfly bush's flower spikes are an irresistible lure to butterflies and hummingbirds all summer long. The plants have an arching habit that's appealing especially as a background in large containers. In warmer climates, butterfly bushes develop rugged trunks that peel. To nurture butterfly bush through cold northern winters, plant in the garden at the end of summer and spread mulch up to 6 inches deep around the trunk. Plants will die down, but resprout in late spring. Prune to the ground to encourage new growth and a more fountainlike shape. Avoid fertilizing butterfly bush; extra-fertile soil fosters leafy growth rather than flower spikes. Remove spent flower spikes to encourage new shoots and flower buds.

Varieties

1 'ADONIS BLUE'
Buddleja davidii 'Adonis Blue' is a dwarf selection with big clusters of dark purple blooms. It grows 5 feet tall and wide. Zones 5–9

2 'BLACK KNIGHT'
Buddleja davidii 'Black Knight' bears flowers of the deepest purple-black all season. In the ground, it grows 10 feet tall and 15 feet wide. Zones 6–9

CONTAINER COMPANIONS

LANTANA
The rounded multiflowered heads of lantana look stunning with the spired blooms of butterfly bush. Both attract butterflies in droves.

CATMINT
Plant a cloud of baby-blue catmint beneath a potted butterfly bush to attract multiple species of butterflies.

DAISY
The starry blooms of daisies make a bright underplanting for butterfly bush.

Calibrachoa
Calibrachoa selections

Type: **Annual**
Height: **5–10 inches tall**
Width: **12–14 inches wide**
Color: **Pink, terra-cotta, yellow, blue, cherry, orange**
Bloom Time: **Summer through fall**

Like a tiny petunia on steroids, calibrachoa (also called million bells) grows and flowers at an amazing rate. Often confused for a petunia, million bells makes a splash no matter where you put it in the garden. It is perfect for containers or hanging baskets but also can be tucked into the front of a border where it will spill out onto a sidewalk or patio. In fact, it may be the ultimate "spiller" for container gardens as long as you give it ample water and fertilizer, which it needs to fuel its astounding growth.

Varieties

1 'CABARET HOT PINK'
'Cabaret Hot Pink' calibrachoa bears multitudes of bright pink flowers on trailing stems to 8 inches.

2 'CABARET PURPLE GLOW'
'Cabaret Purple Glow' calibrachoa is a trailing selection to 8 inches that tolerates part shade. It grows 12 inches wide.

TEST GARDEN TIP
This "spiller" offers a profusion of bird- and hummingbird-attracting flowers.

CONTAINER COMPANIONS

ANGELONIA
Angelonia's snapdragon-like flowers contrast nicely with calibrachoa's pentunia-shape blossoms.

HEUCHERA
The showy foliage of heuchera makes a perfect midrange mound of color in a container full of calibrachoas.

CREEPING JENNY
The golden foliage of creeping Jenny becomes an intertwining backdrop to calibrachoa's showy blooms.

Canna

Canna selections

Zones: **9–11**
Type: **Bulb**
Height: **2–6 feet tall**
Width: **3 feet wide**
Color: **Yellow, red, orange**
Bloom Time: **Summer through fall**

Cannas bring tropical splendor to gardens in all regions. These bold plants feature clustered, flaglike blooms in a brilliant color array on tall stems. Recent flower breeding has created canna foliage that is even showier than the petals, with variegated leaf combinations of orange, yellow, and greens that glow in the summer sun. Dwarf cannas are also available for container gardening and other small spaces. Cannas are usually grown from tuberous roots, but some newer varieties can also be raised from seed, with flowering guaranteed for the first year. If you garden in a climate colder than Zone 9 (7 for the hardier types of cannas), dig up canna plants and store them bare root for the next season, or overwinter potted specimens indoors.

Varieties

1 'AUSTRALIA'
Canna 'Australia' offers a bold combination of deep purple foliage with crimson flowers. It grows to 5 feet tall. Zones 7–10

2 'CLEOPATRA'
Canna 'Cleopatra' bears lush, broad leaves that accompany stems of clustered bright gold flowers, with an occasional orange bloom. It grows to 4 feet tall. Zones 7–11

CONTAINER COMPANIONS

SWEET POTATO VINE
The chartreuse- and chocolate-leafed sweet potato vine varieties contrast nicely with the striped varieties of cannas.

COSMOS
Bright orange cosmos makes a vibrant addition to a container with orange-flowered cannas.

MARIGOLDS
The upright, short growth habit of orange and yellow marigolds melds well with tall, straight cannas.

Cedar (Dwarf)
Cedrus selections

Zones: **6–9**
Type: **Tree**
Height: **1–3 feet tall**
Width: **1–3 feet wide**
Color: **Green, yellow, blue**
Bloom Time: **Foliage looks good all year.**

Graceful sweeping branches and a natural pyramidal shape are the hallmarks of this exceptionally fragrant evergreen. If given plenty of space, cedars will grow to traffic-stopping perfection to be especially appreciated in the winter landscape. But they are equally stunning in containers. Dwarf varieties can live for years in containers, given the right care. Needle color ranges from yellow-tipped green to the silvery tones of the blue Atlas cedar. All cedars are relatively problem free. When the shrubs outgrow their containers, plant them in your yard.

Varieties

**1 'GOLDEN PROMISE'
JAPANESE CEDAR**
'Golden Promise' is a dwarf cedar that typically grows to a maximum of 1 to 2 feet. It has a roundish shape and purplish tints in winter. Zones 6–9

2 'SPIRALIS' JAPANESE CEDAR
'Spiralis' is a dense shrub with yellowish-green, spirally twisted leaves. It occasionally turns bronzy brown in winter and has reddish peeling bark. Zones 6–9

TEST GARDEN TIP
Cedars dislike wet feet. Make sure containers have adequate drainage.

CONTAINER COMPANIONS

OTHER DWARF CONIFERS
Small conifers planted together in the same container are simply adorable. Choose textures and colors that stand out from each other.

CREEPING HERBS
Plant creeping varieties of herbs, such as prostrate rosemary and creeping thyme, with low-growing cedar varieties.

Chrysanthemum

Chrysanthemum selections

Zones: **5–9**
Type: **Perennial**
Height: **1–3 feet tall**
Width: **1–3 feet wide**
Color: **Yellow, orange, russet, red, white, purple, lilac**
Bloom Time: **Late summer through fall**

Chrysanthemums are a must-have for the fall garden. No other fall flower delivers as much color for as long and as reliably as good ol' mums. Mums liven up the fading fall scene with handsome flowers of nearly all shades and colors. Some varieties have daisy blooms; others may be rounded globes, flat, fringed, quill shape, or spoon shape. They work exceptionally well in container plantings and pots.

Varieties

1 DELANO'
Chrysanthemum 'Delano' is a popular red decorative mum often grown as a container plant.

2 'WANDA LAVENDER'
Chrysanthemum 'Wanda Lavender' offers lovely small clustered lilac flowers.

CONTAINER COMPANIONS

'AUTUMN JOY' SEDUM
'Autumn Joy' sedum pairs well with mums in shades of bronze, lavender, pink, and red.

ASTER
The daisylike blooms of asters peak at the same time as chrysanthemums. Aster blooms are usually smaller than mums, so they add fine texture.

ORNAMENTAL GRASS
Micanthus and other grasses come into their glory in autumn as mums display their beauty.

Cuphea
Cuphea selections

Zones: **10–11**
Type: **Annual**
Height: **1–3 feet tall**
Width: **1–3 feet wide**
Color: **Lilac, orange, red**
Bloom Time: **Summer through fall**

Increasingly available in garden centers, exotic cuphea looks like the tropical native it is. It loves hot, humid weather and will bloom all summer, some types producing cool little tubular flowers in red-hot colors that give it one of its common names—cigar flower. It does well in containers, where you can baby it with rich, moist potting soil and keep it well fertilized. Under these conditions, it will bloom nonstop all summer as long as it gets enough water. Look for a variety of forms; some have curious bat-face-shape flowers; others are more tubular.

Varieties

1 'TINY MICE'
Cuphea llavea 'Tiny Mice' bears crimson red flowers on 18-inch-tall plants.

2 'TOTALLY TEMPTED'
Cuphea llavea 'Totally Tempted' bears large crimson-pink flowers on 12-inch-tall plants.

TEST GARDEN TIP
Keep cuphea well watered during hot weather and it will continue to produce blooms.

CONTAINER COMPANIONS

CROSSANDRA
Create a decidedly tropical feel with these two heat- and sun-loving plants.

LANTANA
Accent cuphea's bright flowers with the festive tones in red, yellow, or orange lantana.

MEXICAN SUNFLOWER
Mexican sunflower's brilliant orange or yellow blooms are a perfect contrast to the more intricate cuphea blooms.

TEST GARDEN TIP

Increase dahlia flower size by removing lateral flower buds; this is called disbudding.

Dahlia

Dahlia selections

Zones: **8–11**
Type: **Tuberous roots; perennial**
Height: **1–6 feet tall**
Width: **1–3 feet wide**
Color: **Red, white, purple, green, yellow, organge**
Bloom Time: **Summer through fall**

Dahlias boast petal-packed flowers in bright shades of pink, red, yellow, orange, purple, and white that are excellent for cutting. Grow them in mixed plantings or alone in their own pots. Feed plants every two weeks; cut flowers to promote branching. Dahlias grow from tuberous roots. In winter store them indoors in a cool, dry place to protect the tuberous roots from frost.

Varieties

1 'BISHOP OF LLANDAFF'
Dahlia 'Bishop of Llandaff' bears dark fiery red blooms shaped like small peonies that glow against deep chocolate foliage. This prize-winning dahlia grows to 50 inches tall. Zones 8–10

2 'SB'S SUNNY'
Dahlia 'SB's Sunny' is an award-winning variety that features layers of lemon yellow petals tightly clustered on a round, pom-pom flower. It grows 4 feet tall. Zones 8–10

CONTAINER COMPANIONS

NASTURTIUMS
Yellow and orange low-growing nasturtiums look stunning beneath tall dahlias in a container.

SWEET POTATO VINE
Dark-leaved dahlias such as 'Bishop of Llandaff' make a colorful pairing with chartreuse- or chocolate-leaved sweet potato vine.

OTHER DAHLIAS
Pair large- and small-scale dahlias in the same container to get a double dose of beautiful summer blooms.

Delphinium
Delphinium selections

Zones: **3–7**
Type: **Perennial**
Height: **1–4 feet tall**
Width: **1–3 feet wide**
Color: **Blue, pink, white, purple**
Bloom Time: **Late spring through summer**

Looking like something out of a storybook, delphiniums are the favorite flowers of many gardeners. They produce luxurious, gravity-defying flower spikes, which tower above substantial mounds of coarse leaves. Small-stature varieties do well in containers—especially in spots where the wind might topple taller types. Plants perform best in cool summer climates with little wind and adequate moisture. They may rebloom if flower stalks are cut back after flowers fade.

Varieties

1 'BLUE BUTTERFLY'
Delphinium grandiflorum 'Blue Butterfly' grows to only 14 inches tall and has deep blue flowers with a hint of purple. Chinese delphinium tolerates heat better than regular delphinium, blooming through most of the summer. Zones 4–7

2 'SUMMER MORNING'
Delphinium grandiflorum 'Summer Morning' is the first true pink variety of Chinese delphinium. It grows only 12–14 inches tall, blooming all summer long on well-branched plants. Zones 4–7

TEST GARDEN TIP
If your container is exposed to wind, stake the delphinium in the container so it doesn't snap off at the stem.

CONTAINER COMPANIONS

BLUE SALVIA
Tall annual blue salvia makes a beautiful blue-on-blue combination with blue delphinium.

PETUNIAS
A bubbling cascade of white petunias is a gorgeous accompaniment to straight-standing delphinium plants.

MARIGOLDS
Yellow and blue flowers are a classic pairing. Perky small marigolds offer bright points of light below taller delphinium blooms.

Dusty Miller
Senecio cineraria

Type: **Annual**
Height: **Up to 2 feet tall**
Width: **Up to 2 feet wide**
Color: **Gray-white leaves**
Bloom time: **Foliage looks good from spring through fall.**

Dusty miller is a favorite because it looks good with everything. The silvery-white color is a great foil for any type of garden blossom, and the fine-textured foliage creates a beautiful contrast against other plants' green foliage. Dusty miller has also earned its place in the garden because it's delightfully easy to grow, withstanding heat and drought like a champion. It looks great with any color of flower, adding a bright element to containers and window boxes.

Varieties

1 'BLAZIN' GLORY'
Senecio cephalophorus 'Blazin' Glory' is a heat- and drought-tolerant selection bearing silvery tongue-shape leaves and bold red flowers in summer. It grows 18 inches tall and wide.

2 'SILVER DUST'
'Silver Dust' has finely cut, silver felty leaves. It produces daisylike yellow flowers.

CONTAINER COMPANIONS

ANGELONIA
Silvery dusty miller really sets off dark purple angelonia varieties.

PETUNIA
For a wonderfully classic combination, try red petunias with dusty miller.

BASIL
Though it's not edible, dusty miller is a great choice to add a touch of color to an herb planter. Mix it with purple basil.

Echeveria
Echeveria selections

Zones: **8–10**
Type: **Perennial**
Height: **2–4 inches tall**
Width: **2–6 inches wide**
Color: **Green, white, gray, blue, pink leaves**
Bloom Time: **Foliage looks good from spring through fall.**

These fleshy, colorful succulents are ideal for low-maintenance container gardening. They are drought-tolerant and can be easily propagated. Leaves are fleshy; some are smooth and others are furry. Varieties can feature a flat look and grow very close to the ground. Other varieties are more upright, offering a mass of spiky-looking leaves. These succulents come in a wide range of colors and textures, which make them ideal mixers in succulent bowls.

Varieties

1 *ECHEVERIA LILACINA*
Echeveria lilacina features pale silvery-pink leaves that form a tight rosette. It bears coral-pink flowers on red stems in spring.

2 'MAUNA LOA'
Echeveria 'Mauna Loa' forms large showy rosettes with frilled leaves that change from green to deep red in the sun.

TEST GARDEN TIP
Plant in well-drained soil amended with sand or small gravel. Echeverias don't like wet feet.

CONTAINER COMPANIONS

YARROW
Low-growing mats of deeply cut leaves covered in silvery hairs makes yarrow and echevaria beautiful container mates.

THRIFT
Thrift grows in tight mounds of grassy blue-gray leaves and intertwines with echeveria varieties.

SEDUM
Groundcover sedum varieties thrive in hot, dry spots and offer textural and colorful leaves that complement or contrast with echeveria.

Fanflower

Scaevola aemula

Type: **Annual**
Height: **4–9 inches tall**
Width: **18 inches wide**
Color: **Lavender-blue, white**
Bloom Time: **Summer through fall**

With such pretty blue flowers, you'd think this annual would be rather fussy or delicate. Instead, this durable Australian native takes the heat without wilting and produces an abundance of fanlike lavender-blue or white blooms all summer. It's ideal for cascading from those pots and baskets in hot, dry spots that are difficult to keep watered.

Varieties

1 'BOMBAY DARK BLUE'
Five-petaled half flowers in a rich clear blue make this fanflower a great choice as a solo or companion plant in a container.

2 'DIAMOND'
This lilac-and-white fanflower grows 6 to 8 inches tall and spreads 8 to 15 inches. Elegant and covered with bloom, this annual offers consistent color all summer.

CONTAINER COMPANIONS

SALVIA
Fanflower planted in a container along with blue salvia makes a dramatic display in hot, full sun.

GERBERA DAISY
Fanflower's soft blue-purple blooms complement the bold reds, oranges, yellows, and hot pinks of gerbera daisy.

GERANIUM
Geranium's upright habit combines beautifully with fanflower's soft cascading form.

Feather Grass
Stipa tenuissima

Zones: **7–11**
Type: **Perennial**
Height: **2 feet tall**
Width: **4 feet wide**
Color: **Yellow, tan, green**
Bloom Time: **Foliage looks great from spring through fall.**

Spangled with dew in the morning or after a light shower, the silvery flower panicles of feather grasses light up a garden. Fine-textured Mexican feather grass dances at the slightest puff of wind, providing movement like a billowing wave.

Gardeners may want to plant this self-seeding grass in containers rather than in the garden. It is extremely drought-tolerant, and pests all but ignore it. It offers a lovely natural backdrop for other more-colorful plants.

The grass forms a cascading fountain of foliage. Slender, wiry leaves are green and silky in the spring and turn to a buff color in winter. You may want to leave this grass in a container all winter to enjoy it as winter interest.

CONTAINER COMPANIONS

FALSE SUNFLOWER
The cream daisies of false sunflower meld with the fine texture of Mexican feather grass.

SEDUM
Stiff purple stems and flattish heads of pink flowers of 'Matrona' sedum play off well against delicate Mexican feather grass.

STOKE'S ASTER
The lavender-blue, bachelor's-button-type flowers of Stoke's aster bloom over the same period as feather grass and they make fine companions.

TEST GARDEN TIP
Plant containers of feather grass in an area that is exposed to wind so you can enjoy its kinetic effect.

TEST GARDEN TIP

Fountain grass enjoys full sun but can tolerate some light shade.

Fountain Grass

Pennisetum selections

Zones: **6–11**
Type: **Annual, perennial**
Height: **10 inches to 5 feet tall**
Width: **1–4 feet wide**
Colors: **Green, burgundy foliage; plumes are white, pink, or red**
Bloom Time: **Summer through fall**

Like so many grasses, fountain grass is spectacular when backlit by the rising or setting sun. Named for its especially graceful spray of foliage, fountain grass also sends out beautiful fuzzy flower plumes in late summer.

The white, pink, or red plumes (depending on variety) continue into fall and bring a loose, informal look to plantings. Leave this showy grass in its container for the winter and you'll enjoy its architectural shape frosted with ice or dusted with snow.

This plant self-seeds freely, sometimes to the point of becoming invasive. If you are worried about self-seeding, remove the seed heads before they mature. They make excellent additions to cut flower bouquets.

CONTAINER COMPANIONS

DAYLILY
Colorful daylily flowers contrast beautifully with fountain grass. They thrive in the same conditions.

FALSE SUNFLOWER
Brilliant daisy flowers of false sunflower are cooled by softly waving fountain grass.

DAHLIA
Dahlia flowers lose some of their stiff formality when planted alongside fountain grass.

Geranium

Pelargonium selections

Zones: **10–11**
Type: **Annual, perennial**
Height: **2 feet tall**
Width: **2 feet wide**
Colors: **Red, pink, white, purple**
Bloom Time: **Summer through fall**

Geraniums have been a gardener's favorite for well over a century. The old-fashioned standard for containers (and also beds and borders), geranium is still one of the most popular plants today. Traditional types love hot weather and hold up well to dry conditions; many also offer colorful foliage. Regal, also called Martha Washington, geraniums are more delicate-looking and do better in the cool conditions of spring and fall. Though most geraniums are grown as annuals, they are perennials in Zones 10–11. Bring them indoors to overwinter, if you like, then replant in containers outdoors in spring after the threat of frost has passed. They can bloom indoors all year long if they get enough light.

Varieties

1 'AMERICANA BRIGHT RED'
Pelargonium 'Americana Bright Red' is a heat-loving geranium with large, rich red flower heads. It grows 18 inches tall.

2 'ALLURE LIGHT PINK'
Pelargonium 'Allure Light Pink' bears pink petals with a brighter pink blotch on vigorous plants that grow 18 inches tall.

TEST GARDEN TIP
Pinch back the blooms from geraniums in early spring to promote branching.

CONTAINER COMPANIONS

FLOWERING TOBACCO
Use flowering tobacco to add sweet fragrance to your planting of geraniums.

PENTAS
With its large heads of colorful flowers, pentas looks great with geranium—and appreciates the same growing conditions.

FOUNTAIN GRASS
Enhance geranium's form with the texture and rich color of purple fountain grass.

Gloriosa Daisy
Rudbeckia hirta

Zones: **4–9**
Type: **Perennial**
Height: **1–3 feet tall**
Width: **1 foot wide**
Color: **Yellow, red, orange**
Bloom Time: **Summer through fall**

A member of the black-eyed Susan family, gloriosa daisy is showier than its cousins, boasting large, brightly colored, dark-eyed blooms in shades of red, orange, or yellow. Heat- and drought-tolerant, these robust growers flower from June through September with regular deadheading. 'Irish Eyes', 1½ to 2 feet tall, sports yellow flowers with green centers.

Varieties

1 *RUDBECKIA HIRTA* 'IRISH EYES'
A tender perennial that occasionally returns for an encore the following year, 'Irish Eyes' is best treated as an annual flower. It's named for the green eye of its daisylike bloom. Its height and habit make it look like a perennial, but it blooms nonstop all summer. It's not fussy about watering once established.

2 'TIGER EYE GOLD'
'Tiger Eye Gold' features 4-inch-wide semi-double flowers. Glowing orange-gold petals surround a brown button center. Plants bloom all season long.

CONTAINER COMPANIONS

FOUNTAIN GRASS
The arching leaves and bottlebrush flower spikelets of fountain grass combine well with the upright blooms of gloriosa daisy.

RUSSIAN SAGE
Russian sage produces sprays of purple flowers borne on long stems that look stunning next to the sunny yellow blooms of gloriosa daisy.

Gooseneck Loosestrife
Lysimachia selections

Zones: **4–9**
Type: **Perennial**
Height: **2 inches to 4 feet tall**
Width: **1–2 feet wide**
Color: **White, yellow, green**
Bloom Time: **Summer through fall**

Loosestrife is a vigorous grower and a beautiful addition to containers. Loosestrife forms vary from tall, stately plants, such as gooseneck loosestrife (*Lysimachia clethroides*), to others that can be planted as creeping or trailing container additions. Flowers, too, vary from tight spikes of ½-inch to 1-inch cups carried alone or in whorls. Humus-rich, moisture-retentive soil is recommended; some varieties enjoy wet soil and ample water. Several sorts may become invasive and need to be corralled. These are not the invasive purple loosestrife, which has been banned in many parts of the United States.

Varieties

1 CIRCLE FLOWER
Lysimachia punctata, or whorled loosestrife, has 1-inch yellow flowers along the upper part of leafy 3-foot stems. The dark 3-inch leaves, sometimes variegated with white, are also arranged in whorls. Zones 4–8

2 GOLDEN CREEPING JENNY
Lysimachia nummularia 'Aurea' is a fast-growing groundcover for shade or partial shade. It bears round chartreuse foliage and grows 2 inches tall. It can spread indefinitely. Zones 4–8

TEST GARDEN TIP
Gooseneck loosestrife can become invasive. Growing it in a container is a great way to control it.

CONTAINER COMPANIONS

HELENIUM
Bronzy varieties of helenium blend well with the purple form of hairy loosestrife.

CALLA
In wet places in mild regions, white calla lily is a surprising but effective companion for yellow loosestrife. The flower forms are in dramatic contrast with each other, and they enjoy similar conditions.

TEST GARDEN TIP

Heleniums produce additional blooms by deadheading. Remove spent flowers as they fade.

Helenium

Helenium selections

Zones: **3–8**
Type: **Perennial**
Height: **2–5 feet tall**
Width: **1–2 feet wide**
Color: **Yellow**
Bloom Time: **Summer through fall**

Long-blooming helenium lights up a late-season container garden with showy daisy flowers in brilliant yellows, browns, and mahogany, centered with prominent yellow or brown disks. Many of the best cultivars are hybrids. All are excellent for cutting. Deadhead to extend bloom time and divide the clumps every couple of years to ensure vigor.

Varieties

1 'BUTTERPAT'
Helenium 'Butterpat' grows to 4 feet or even taller with bright yellow ray flowers and a prominent yellow disk. Zones 4–8

2 'MARDI GRAS'
Helenium 'Mardi Gras' bears 2-inch daisies in rich orange washed with yellow and red. Its upright clumps may reach 3 feet tall. Zones 4–8

CONTAINER COMPANIONS

OBEDIENT PLANT
Upright flower spikes of obedient plant contrast well with the flat daisy flower of helenium.

DAYLILY
Daylily's red, yellow, and gold trumpet flowers echo the colors of helenium but with a different flower shape. They thrive in similar conditions.

MONKSHOOD
Brilliant blue monkshood makes a striking complementary impact against helenium's orange and gold.

Hibiscus
Hibiscus selections

Zones: **6–11**
Type: **Perennial**
Height: **4–10 feet tall**
Width: **3–5 feet wide**
Color: **White, pink, red**
Bloom Time: **Summer through fall**

Hibiscus flowers might be the most dramatic in the garden and can bloom as large as a child's head in gorgeous colors. The hibiscus plant itself is large and dramatic, and it needs plenty of space to show off. Plant it in large containers and place in a sunny location where this plant can really show off. Although the huge funnel-shape flowers seldom last more than a day, they are abundant and the plant blooms over several weeks. The large leaves tend to draw Japanese beetles. Hibiscus needs plenty of water, so grow it in rich, loose, well-drained soil where you can water it easily and regularly during dry spells.

Varieties

1 'BLUE RIVER II'
Hibiscus moscheutos 'Blue River II' shows off 10-inch-wide, pure white blooms on 6-foot stems in midsummer to fall. Zones 5–10

2 'FIREBALL'
'Fireball' is one of the most stunning perennial hibiscus. It bears bold red flowers to 12 inches across on 5-foot-tall stems. It grows 3 feet wide. Zones 5–9

TEST GARDEN TIP
Plant several containers of hibiscus to create a colorful privacy hedge at the edge of a deck or patio.

CONTAINER COMPANIONS

JOE PYE WEED
Joe Pye weed matches hibiscus in stature and bears heads of dusty-rose flowers to contrast to the bold funnel-shape of hibiscus blooms.

MISCANTHUS
Tall miscanthus planted among hibiscus presents a natural-looking scene.

TURTLEHEAD
The tubular pink or white flowers of turtlehead are good companions for hibiscus.

Iceplant
Delosperma selections

Zones: **5–10**
Type: **Perennial**
Height: **4–8 inches tall**
Width: **1–2 feet wide**
Color: **Pink, purple, yellow**
Bloom Time: **Spring through fall**

This is a great colorful flower for any container. Iceplant produces attractive green, needlelike succulent foliage that becomes covered with purplish-pink or yellow flowers at peak bloom. Enjoy iceplant's blooms in late spring to early summer. Hardy iceplant needs full sun and excellent drainage to do well.

Varieties

1 COOPER'S HARDY

Delosperma cooperi forms a mat of creeping succulent foliage several inches tall by 2 feet wide. It has hot pink daisylike flowers. Zones 5–10

2 YELLOW ICEPLANT

This lovely and rugged iceplant forms a semi-evergreen rug. Plants love hot sun and dry conditions.

CONTAINER COMPANIONS

COREOPSIS

The airy yellow daisies of 'Moonbeam' coreopsis look outstanding dancing above a carpet of hardy iceplant.

VERONICA

The upright spires of veronica creates a striking contrast to the low, creeping mat of hardy iceplant.

SEDUM

The succulent foliage of 'Blue Spruce' sedum mimics that of hardy iceplant.

Kale and Ornamental Cabbage

Brassica oleracea selections

Zones: **5–10**
Type: **Annual**
Height: **12–18 inches tall**
Width: **1–2 feet wide**
Color: **Purple, pink, white, green**
Bloom Time: **Summer through fall**

Thank goodness for kale. It's one of the few plants available to add a fresh burst of color and life to the fall containers. Its leaves come with beautiful variegations in pinks, purples, and reds that blend beautifully with changing autumn foliage. Plant it in spring or in the fall after you tear out tired or frost-damaged annuals such as marigolds and impatiens. It likes rich, well-drained but moist potting mix.

Varieties

1 'CHIDORI WHITE'
Brassica 'Chidori White' offers blue-green heads with large, bright, creamy white centers.

2 'PEACOCK RED'
Brassica 'Peacock Red' offers feathery leaves with rich purple-red centers.

TEST GARDEN TIP
The heads of ornamental cabbage get so large that they can go solo in a container.

CONTAINER COMPANIONS

LEADWORT
Add ornamental kale to a border with leadplant for a stunning pairing. Leadplant's blue flowers look great against gray-green kale leaves; then leadplant's leaves turn red and add another dimension of interest.

CHRYSANTHEMUM
These two fall classics combine beautifully. Yellow and red mums are great picks to add an extra shot of interest to pink and purple kale varieties.

TEST GARDEN TIP

Lantana are butterfly magnets. Watch for swallowtails and monarchs who are drawn to the flowers.

Lantana

Lantana selections

Zones: **9–11**
Type: **Annual, perennial**
Height: **Up to 4 tall**
Width: **Up to 4 feet wide**
Color: **White, blue, purple, orange, red, yellow, bicolors**
Bloom Time: **Summer through fall**

If you have a hot, baked spot, lantana is your answer. This hardworking plant not only thrives with little moisture and in full, unyielding sun, it does so with ease. In fact, lantana is a flower that seems to have it all: It produces an abundance of brightly colored flowers all summer and fall, and it's attractive to butterflies (hummingbirds like it too). It's easy to grow and a great choice for containers. Plus, if you have a sunny spot indoors, you can grow it as a charming indoor plant. In frost-free climates (Zones 9–11), it's a great perennial groundcover as well.

Varieties

1 'BANDANA CHERRY'
Lantana 'Bandana Cherry' offers rich yellow, orange, and cherry red blooms in large heads.

2 'IRENE'
Lantana 'Irene' bears bright yellow, pink, and red blooms in large clusters on a spreading plant.

CONTAINER COMPANIONS

ANGELONIA
Since lantana has a spreading habit, grow it with an upright plant, such as angelonia, to add height and variation to your plantings.

PENTAS
Colorful pentas heads attract tons of butterflies and hummingbirds, and they like hot, dry spots, much like lantana.

SALVIA
Many types of salvia, especially blue salvia, look great with the fiery-color cultivars of lantana.

Lemongrass

Cymbopogon citratus

Zones: **9–11**
Type: **Perennial, herb**
Height: **3–6 feet tall**
Width: **2–3 feet wide**
Color: **Green leaves**
Bloom Time: **Foliage looks good from spring through fall.**

Grow a touch of the tropics by tucking a clump of lemongrass into a pot or garden bed. This herb brings the textural beauty and movement of an ornamental grass to the garden, along with one additional feature: lemony leaves with a hint of ginger. Lemongrass leaps out of the ground when warm nights arrive. Watch for fresh stalks to emerge.

Combine lemongrass with cilantro, chile peppers, and garlic for the makings of Thai and Asian cuisine. In cold regions, dig a side stalk in late summer and plunk it into a pot to grow indoors through winter.

The long, grassy foliage of lemongrass is the perfect center-of-the-container star. It grows several feet tall and can be harvested all summer for soups and pasta dishes.

CONTAINER COMPANIONS

LEMON THYME

Fragrant and flavorful lemon thyme is an excellent container mate for lemongrass. Most herbs thrive best in well-drained conditions—as both these herbs do.

LEMON VERBENA

Plant a smorgasbord of lemony foliage by interplanting lemon verbena with lemongrass. Clip leaves of both and steep in hot water for delicious lemony tea.

TEST GARDEN TIP

Lemongrass is a tall, leafy plant that can be used as the focal point in a container.

Licorice Plant
Helichrysum selections

Type: **Annual, perennial**
Height: **1–2 feet tall**
Width: **1–2 feet wide**
Color: **Silvery white leaves**
Bloom Time: **Foliage looks good from spring through fall.**

Elegant silvery licorice plant is so useful to set off flowers in blue, white, purple, and other colors and to add contrast to plantings where you want more than just a mass of green. It's especially good in containers, where you can admire it up close and show off its spreading habit to best effect. Technically a tropical shrub, licorice plant is usually grown as an annual in the United States. It does best in full sun and well-drained potting mix.

Varieties

1 'ICICLES'
Helichrysum 'Icicles' bears threadlike silvery foliage on upright 2-foot-tall plants.

2 'LEMON LICORICE'
Helichrysum 'Lemon Licorice' bears silvery chartreuse foliage and can grow to 2 feet wide in containers.

CONTAINER COMPANIONS

ANGELONIA
Set off rich purple angelonia flowers with licorice plant's silvery foliage.

GERBERA DAISY
Create a charming pairing with white or pastel gerbera daisy and licorice plant.

ORNAMENTAL PEPPER
Put together a stunning contrast with purple-leaf ornamental peppers and silvery licorice plant.

Marguerite Daisy
Argyranthemum selections

Type: **Annual**
Height: **1–2 feet tall**
Width: **1–2 feet wide**
Color: **White, pink, or yellow**
Bloom Time: **Summer**

For a spectacular show during cool weather, plant marguerite daisy. Often confused with shasta daisy, marguerite is more mounded and shrubby. Different types also come in pink with a bloom that more resembles purple coneflower. Marguerite daisy's hallmark is that it loves cool weather—and blooms best in most areas in spring and fall, though it will continue to bloom through the summer in mild-summer areas. Even when it's not in bloom, the dark green, finely cut foliage looks good against just about any light-color flower.

Varieties

1 'FIREBALL RED'
Argyranthemum 'Fireball Red' offers double red flowers on a 1-foot-tall plant.

2 'MADEIRA PINK'
Argyranthemum 'Madeira Pink' offers double pink flowers on 1-foot-tall plants.

TEST GARDEN TIP
Plant spring containers with this cool-weather annual. Replace with heat-loving annuals in summer.

CONTAINER COMPANIONS

DIANTHUS
Create old-fashioned charm by mixing a pot of these daisy-shape flowers with pink dianthus.

LARKSPUR
Pair marguerite daisy with spires of purple larkspur for a stunning display. The flowers work well together in bouquets.

NEMESIA
Marguerite daisy's larger flowers look beautiful against the smaller, more delicate nemesia blooms.

TEST GARDEN TIP

At the end of the growing season, let flowers form seed heads and save seeds for next year's containers.

Marigold
Tagetes patula

Type: **Annual**
Height: **8–12 inches tall**
Width: **6–8 inches wide**
Color: **Orange, yellow, red, white**
Bloom Time: **Summer through fall**

Just as you'd expect from something called French, *Tagetes patula* is the fancy marigold. French marigolds tend to be frilly and some boast a distinctive "crested eye." They grow roughly 8–12 inches tall with a chic, neat growth habit and elegant dark green foliage. They do best in full sun with moist, well-drained potting soil and will flower all summer long. Their seeds are easy to collect and save for potting up next season.

Varieties

1 'DISCO QUEEN'
Tagetes patula 'Disco Queen' bears orange-red flowers ringed in yellow on long-blooming plants that grow 1 foot tall and wide.

2 'DURANGO RED'
Tagetes patula 'Durango Red' produces orange-red flowers all summer long on plants that grow 1 foot tall and wide.

CONTAINER COMPANIONS

BIDENS
Bidens is such a rugged plant, it'll bloom happily while draped across hot pavement. It's great along a front edge with marigolds standing up behind.

MOSS ROSE
Charming moss roses make a colorful, carefree carpet underneath French marigolds.

ZINNIA
It takes bold blooms to hold their own next to marigolds, and zinnias are ready for the job.

Nasturtium

Tropaeolum selections

Type: **Annual, vine**
Height: **Mounding varieties from 9 to 16 inches tall; climbing varieties from 3 to 15 feet.**
Width: **12–18 inches wide**
Color: **Orange, white, yellow**
Bloom Time: **Summer through fall**

Nasturtiums are so versatile. They grow easily from seed and bloom all season until frost; they are never greedy about food or fertilizer. Nasturtiums are available in either spreading or climbing types. Plant spreading types in large containers to spill over the sides. Train climbing types up trellises in containers. The leaves and flowers are edible; use them as a showy plate garnish or to jazz up salads.

Varieties

1 'ALASKA'
Tropaeolum majus 'Alaska' is a trailing variety to 12 to 15 inches. It offers exciting, white-splashed foliage and striking red, orange, gold, yellow, and salmon flowers.

2 'EMPRESS OF INDIA'
Tropaeolum majus 'Empress of India' bears velvety, crimson-red flowers on a compact, 14-inch-tall plant.

TEST GARDEN TIP
Harvest the peppery-flavor edible blooms of nasturtiums and add them to salads and soups.

CONTAINER COMPANIONS

PETUNIA
Any color petunia can accompany neutral creamy-color nasturtiums; many of the pink petunias combine well with dark burgundy nasturtiums.

COSMOS
Cherry red nasturtiums glow warmly when planted alongside pure white cosmos.

FRENCH MARIGOLD
Pure orange or yellow marigolds make tidy edging plants for a pot of nasturtiums.

Nemesia
Nemesia selections

Type: **Annual**
Height: **Up to 2 feet**
Width: **Up to 1 foot wide**
Color: **Pink, blue, white**
Bloom Time: **Spring through fall**

Nemesia is a charming cool-season annual with pretty little snapdragon-shape flowers—often fragrant—that bloom in a wide range of colors. It does best in spring and fall (winter in mild-winter climates), though some varieties have better heat tolerance than others. In cool-summer areas, such as the Pacific Northwest, nemesia will continue to bloom right through the summer into fall. Nemesia prefers moist, well-drained potting soil that's rich in organic matter.

Varieties

1 'AROMATICA TRUE BLUE'
Nemesia 'Aromatica True Blue' bears fragrant soft-blue flowers on 14-inch-tall plants.

2 'SERENGETI RED'
Nemesia 'Serengeti Red' is an especially eye-catching selection with deep red flowers. It grows 10 inches tall.

CONTAINER COMPANIONS

DIANTHUS
Create a container of fragrant delights by pairing nemesia with scented dianthus varieties.

SNAPDRAGON
Mix mounding nemesia with soft shades of upright snapdragon for a lovely spring combination.

PANSY
Charming violas mix beautifully with nemesias, especially the smaller-flowering types.

New Zealand Flax

Phormium selections

Zones: **9–11**
Type: **Annual, perennial**
Height: **3–4 feet tall**
Width: **3–4 feet wide**
Color: **Red, yellow, or green flowers, depending on variety**
Bloom Time: **Summer**

Bring a note of the tropics to your garden with the bold, colorful, strappy leaves of New Zealand flax. They are excellent as container plants that can be overwintered with protection. Flower panicles may reach 12 feet tall in some selections with red or yellow tubular flowers. Blooms appear only in mild climates, but there they attract many species of birds. If space is limited, check out dwarf forms. While New Zealand flax is a popular perennial in frost-free areas, it's becoming more and more loved in northern regions, where it's treated as an annual.

Varieties

1 'SUNSET'

Phormium 'Sunset' is an upright 5-foot flax with 1½-inch-wide leaves. These are bright pinkish red, striped with olive especially along the margins. Zones 9–11

2 'DARK DELIGHT'

Phormium 'Dark Delight' has evergreen 1- to 2-inch-wide strap-shape leaves in dull purple. This hybrid has leaves 4 feet long. Zones 9–11

TEST GARDEN TIP
Think big when you choose containers for phormium because this showy foliage plant spreads out.

CONTAINER COMPANIONS

PHLOX
The pure white flower clusters of 'David' phlox show off dramatically against dwarf forms of deep-red-leaved New Zealand flax in sun.

SUNFLOWERS
Sunflowers are a gorgeous match for New Zealand flax. Its bright yellow petals contrast well with dark leaves.

DAHLIA
Tall yellow, pink, bronze, or red dahlias are fine companions for New Zealand flax.

TEST GARDEN TIP
At the end of the growing season, plant container oreganos directly into the garden.

Oregano
Origanum vulgare

Zones: **5–11**
Type: **Perennial, herb**
Height: **1–2 feet tall**
Width: **2–4 feet wide**
Color: **White pinkish-purple blooms**
Bloom Time: **Summer**

Savor true Italian flavor with garden-fresh oregano. This sprawling herb pumps up the taste in tomato sauces, pizza, and Mediterranean cuisine. An easy-growing perennial, oregano thrives in planting beds or containers. Plant it in a pot with rosemary, sage, and thyme for a flavorful quartet you can place near the kitchen door, handy for snipping and sprinkling into sauces, soups, and stews. In the ground, plants will flower and set seed, which shortens the harvest season. Pinch flowers from stems to keep plants in top snipping form.

Varieties

1 GOLDEN OREGANO
Origanum vulgare 'Aureum', or golden oregano, is a vigorous creeping oregano with small rounded leaves. In early or later summer, golden oregano produces small pink or lavender to purple flowers. Zones 5–9

2 GREEK OREGANO
Origanum vulgaris hirtum, or Greek oregano, grows 2 feet tall and bears dark green leaves topped with white flowers in summer. Clip it often because it offers intense flavor. Zones 5–9

CONTAINER COMPANIONS

THYME
Thyme's low-growing, small rounded leaves contrast nicely with oregano.

BASIL
Grow small-leafed basil such as 'Spicy Globe' with oregano in a container. Clip leaves often and use in Italian dishes such as pasta and pizza.

PATIO TOMATOES
Small-stature tomatoes make a great pairing with oregano planted at the base. Both love hot, sunny spots and can be harvested and served together.

Pentas
Pentas lanceolata

Zones: **10–11**
Type: **Annual, perennial**
Height: **Up to 4 feet tall**
Width: **Up to 3 feet wide**
Bloom Time: **Spring through fall**

Pentas is one of the best butterfly-attracting plants around. It blooms all summer long, even during the hottest weather, with large clusters of starry blooms that attract butterflies by the dozens as well as hummingbirds. The plant grows well in containers and in the ground—and it can even make a good houseplant if you have enough light. It does best in full sun and moist, well-drained soil. Pentas is grown as an annual in most parts of the country, but it's hardy in Zones 10–11. Plant it outdoors after all danger of frost has passed.

Varieties

1 'BUTTERFLY LIGHT LAVENDER'
Pentas 'Butterfly Light Lavender' bears lavender-pink flower heads on compact 14-inch-tall plants.

2 'GRAFFITI WHITE'
Pentas 'Graffiti White' bears large flower heads of pure white blooms on 12-inch-tall plants.

TEST GARDEN TIP
Pentas also makes a long-lasting cut flower. Cut extra blooms for indoor bouquets.

CONTAINER COMPANIONS

LANTANA
Multicolor lantana flowers add bright shades to pentas—and both plants are butterfly magnets.

SALVIA
Both pentas and salvia love hot weather and are surefire picks for butterflies and hummingbirds.

AFRICAN MARIGOLD
Complement pentas' bright flowers with bold yellow marigolds for a big-impact, low-care combination.

Petunia

Petunia selections

Zones: 10–11
Type: **Annual**
Height: **6 inches to 4 feet long**
Width: **1–4 feet wide**
Color: **Pink, white, purple, black, yellow, orange, blue**
Bloom Time: **Spring through fall**

Petunias are failproof favorites for gardeners everywhere. They are vigorous growers and prolific bloomers from midspring through late fall. Color choices are nearly limitless, with some sporting beautiful veining and intriguing colors. Many varieties are sweetly fragrant. Some also tout themselves as "weatherproof," which means that the flowers don't close up when water is splashed on them. Wave petunias have made this annual even more popular. Reaching up to 4 feet long, they cascade from window boxes and pots. All petunias do best and grow more bushy and full if you pinch or cut them back by one- to two-thirds in midsummer.

Varieties

1 'CASCADIAS BICOLOR PURPLE'
Petunia 'Cascadias Bicolor Purple' is a heavy-blooming variety bearing purple flowers with a white star in the center. It has a trailing habit.

2 'SWEET SUNSHINE COMPACT NOSTALGIA'
Petunia 'Sweet Sunshine Compact Nostalgia' shows off beautiful, soft pink double flowers touched with creamy yellow on a 14-inch mounding plant.

CONTAINER COMPANIONS

SWEET ALYSSUM
Tiny, delicate alyssum contrasts well with the much larger blooms of petunia.

HELIOTROPE
Heliotrope and sprawling petunias combine beautifully in containers, creating a fragrant magnet for butterflies.

SALVIA
Upright salvias in purple, red, or white create a regal backdrop behind ground-creeping petunias.

Purple Heart
Setcreasea pallida

Zones: **8–11**
Type: **Annual**
Height: **6–12 inches long**
Width: **1–3 feet wide**
Color: **Purple foliage**
Bloom Time: **Foliage looks good from spring to fall.**

Purple heart gets its name from its dark foliage. Give it star power in hanging baskets or as a container edging contrasted with taller chartreuse foliage plants. Also known as *Tradescantia pallida*, it produces pale pink flowers from midsummer to early fall. The plant grows best in full sun or light shade and loses its purple hue in too much shade. Fertilize once a month.

Varieties

1 'PALE PUMA'
Setcreasea pallida 'Pale Puma' produces masses of fleshy purple stems covered with leaves that are green in the center with purple toward the edges. Bright sun makes the leaves deeper purple. Zones 7–10

2 'PURPLE QUEEN'
Setcreasea pallida 'Purple Queen' has long strappy leaves colored red to burgundy. Plants are topped with pink flowers. Zones 8–10

TEST GARDEN TIP
In spring, pinch the tips of purple heart to encourage lusher, fuller growth.

CONTAINER COMPANIONS

MONEYWORT
The chartreuse hues of trailing moneywort pair well with purple heart in containers and window boxes.

ANGELONIA
White lacy blooms of angelonia look stunning next to the spearlike dark purple leaves of purple heart.

PHORMIUM
Spiky purple phormiums paired with trailing purple heart make a beautiful all-purple container or window box.

Rose
Rosa selections

Zones: **4–9**
Type: **Rose**
Height: **1–6 feet tall**
Width: **1–3 feet wide**
Color: **Red, fuchsia, white, pink, yellow, orange, salmon, bicolors**
Bloom Time: **Spring through fall**

Roses are sold in a wide range of sizes that make them perfect container plants. Standard or tree roses grow well in large containers and can make a beautiful and fragrant entryway welcome when planted in matching containers and flanking a doorway. Small shrub roses grow well in containers as well, providing gorgeous flowers and foliage. Miniature roses are ideal for small containers. Roses require a sunny location. At the end of the season, plant roses in the ground and mulch well.

Varieties

1 'THE FAIRY'

'The Fairy', a Polyantha rose, blooms nonstop from June until frost. Small, rosette-shape double flowers are sweet light pink. It grows 2 to 3 feet high and wide and will take some shade. Zones 5–9

2 'GREEN ICE' MINIATURE ROSE

'Green Ice' is a miniature rose that grows about 18 inches tall and wide. It produces small apricot buds that open into cool green double blooms that deepen in color when grown in partial shade). Zones 5–9

CONTAINER COMPANIONS

LAVENDER
The gray-green foliage of lavender makes a nice companion for dark-green-leafed roses.

ALYSSUM
Lacy white alyssum looks stunning tumbling out of a pot filled with blooming red or pink roses.

MINIATURE ROSES
Pair large and small (miniature) roses together in the same container.

Sage
Salvia officinalis

Zones: **4–10**
Type: **Perennial, herb**
Height: **12–24 inches tall**
Width: **24–36 inches**
Color: **Mauve, rose-purple blend, white**
Bloom Time: **Summer**

You just can't overdo sage in containers. This perennial herb earns its keep with fast-growing ways, beautiful blooms, and fine flavor. Once established, plants shrug off drought, although it's wise to keep plants well-hydrated through the hottest parts of summer if you want a steady supply of supple foliage. Pinch out flower buds to keep leaves forming. Or allow them to form and enjoy the flowers in containers. Besides its popular use as a culinary herb, sage is also commonly pressed into service in cosmetics, perfumes, and soaps. It can be enjoyed in all herb planters or mixed in with colorful annuals.

Varieties

1 'BERGGARTEN'
Salvia officinalis 'Berggarten' produces large, round gray-green leaves that are more flavorful than common sage. It grows 2 feet tall and wide. Zones 5–8

2 'TRICOLOR'
Salvia officinalis 'Tricolor' has foliage splashed with green, cream, and purple; in sunniest locations, the cream deepens to pink. Zones 6–11

TEST GARDEN TIP
Mix different colors of sage (purple, green, golden) together in the same pot.

CONTAINER COMPANIONS

LANTANA
Sage and lantana both love sunny spots and can take dry soil. Combine yellow lantana with golden sage.

THYME
Low-growing thymes make excellent pot mates with sage. Plant other herbs to create a kitchen garden in a pot.

MARIGOLDS
Perky yellow or orange marigolds blend nicely with green and golden sage.

Snapdragon
Antirrhinum majus

Type: **Annual**
Height: **1–4 feet tall**
Width: **6–12 inches tall**
Color: **Red, pink, yellow, orange, white**
Bloom Time: **Spring through fall**

The easy charm of snapdragons can add color to almost any container planting in spring or fall. They get their name from the fact that you can gently squeeze the sides of the intricately shaped flower and see the jaws of a dragon head snap closed. The blooms come in gorgeous colors, including some with beautiful color variations on each flower. Plus, snapdragons are an outstanding cut flower. Gather a dozen or more in a small vase and you'll have one of the prettiest bouquets around. Snapdragons are especially useful because they're a cool-season annual, coming into their own in early spring when the warm-season annuals, such as marigolds and impatiens, are just being planted.

Varieties

1 'BUTTERFLY BRONZE'
Antirrhinum 'Bronze Butterfly' bears open-faced, golden-orange flowers on 3-foot-tall plants.

2 'ROCKET RED'
Antirrhinum 'Rocket Red' bears crimson-red flowers on 3-foot-tall stems.

CONTAINER COMPANIONS

LICORICE PLANT
The silvery foliage of licorice plant looks good with dark red snapdragons.

PETUNIA
Snapdragons come in about as many colors as petunias, so it's easy to find varieties that look great together.

SALVIA
Another old-fashioned favorite, salvia produces spikes of brightly colored flowers that complement snapdragons perfectly.

Swan River Daisy
Brachyscome selections

Type: **Annual**
Height: **12–18 inches tall**
Width: **6–12 inches wide**
Color: **Violet, pink, white, blue**
Bloom Time: **Summer through fall**

Pretty little starlike flowers combined with ferny green foliage are what make Swan River daisy so popular. It's a top pick to spill lightly over the sides of container plantings and hanging baskets. This cool-season annual does best when planted in spring a few weeks before your region's last frost date. It needs rich, moist, but well-drained potting mix. Deadhead to prolong bloom. When summer's heat hits, shear plants back by about half to rejuvenate them and encourage fall bloom.

Varieties

1 'SURDAISY STRAWBERRY PINK'
Brachyscome 'Surdaisy Strawberry Pink' has clear pink blooms that open against dark green leaves. The plant has a spherical shape.

2 BLUE SWAN RIVER DAISY
Blue-hued Swan River daisy grows 1 to 2 feet tall and wide. It spills over the sides of containers and is covered with a blanket of blue blooms.

TEST GARDEN TIP
Plant in a fertile, well-drained potting soil. Swan River daisies do best in morning sun.

CONTAINER COMPANIONS

GAZANIA
Mix the small blue flowers of Swan River daisy with gazania's bigger, bolder flowers.

GERANIUM
Combine soft pink or white varieties of geranium with Swan River daisy for a soothing combination you can count on throughout the summer.

LISIANTHUS
Swan River daisy looks great with any color of lisianthus. The two plants have contrasting foliage textures to add even more interest.

TEST GARDEN TIP

A relative of morning glories and moonflowers, these vines fill in fast once the weather heats up.

Sweet Potato

Ipomoea batatas

Type: **Annual**
Height: **2 feet tall**
Width: **5 feet wide**
Color: **Green, black, tricolor**
Bloom Time: **Foliage is attractive summer through fall**

Among the most popular container-garden plants, sweet potato vine is a vigorous grower that you can count on to make a big impact. Its colorful foliage in shades of chartreuse or purple accents just about any other plant. Grow a few together in a large pot and they make a big impact all on their own. Sweet potato vines do best during the warm days of summer and prefer moist, well-drained potting mix. They thrive in sun or shade.

Varieties

1 'BLACKIE'

Ipomoea batatas 'Blackie' offers dark purple hand-shape foliage on a vigorous plant.

2 'ILLUSION EMERALD LACE'

Ipomoea batatas 'Illusion Emerald Lace' is a compact selection with bright lime green foliage and a mounding/trailing habit.

CONTAINER COMPANIONS

ANGELONIA
Golden sweet potato vine is a perfect complement to purple angelonia varieties.

MARIGOLDS
Mix orange marigolds with purple sweet potato vine for a combo that looks colorful all summer long.

NEW GUINEA IMPATIENS
Add color to shady spots with purple or orange New Guinea impatiens and golden sweet potato vine.

Thyme
Thymus selections

Zones: **4–9**
Type: **Perennial**
Height: **3–12 inches tall**
Width: **18 inches wide**
Color: **Blue, violet, white**
Bloom Time: **Summer through fall**

Introduce scenery from the Greek Isles to your container garden with lush plantings of thyme. This sun-loving, drought-tolerant herb carpets hillsides in Greece, thriving in well-drained soil. Drought conditions concentrate the aromatic oils in thyme, so the drier your growing conditions, the better. Tuck plants along side other herbs in a container or window box. They look great with flowers too. The flowers beckon honeybees, so add thyme to pots to ensure an ample supply of pollinators.

Varieties

1 ENGLISH THYME
Thymus vulgaris is the classic culinary thyme. It adds a savory note in soups, stews, and sauces. Zones 5–9

2 RED CREEPING THYME
Thymus serpyllum carpets the ground with red blossoms in spring. This groundcover is a natural addition to an alpine or rock garden, or tucked between stepping-stones along a garden path. Zones 4–9

TEST GARDEN TIP
Cut leaves and flowers to use throughout the growing season. The more you cut, the more it will grow.

CONTAINER COMPANIONS

SAGE
Golden sage contrasts nicely with thyme varieties. Both like well-drained soil and do well in full sun.

ROSEMARY
Creeping, or prostrate, rosemary is an excellent mate with thyme. Clip both herbs to add to Italian dishes such as pasta and pizza.

CHAMOMILE
Yellow-flowering chamomile is beautiful when planted with thyme. Clip leaves from both to make herbal teas.

TEST GARDEN TIP

Verbenas do best in a sunny spot planted in well-drained potting soil.

Verbena

Verbena selections

Zones: **7–9**
Type: **Perennial, annual**
Height: **9–18 inches tall**
Width: **12–20 inches wide**
Color: **White, pink, fuchsia, red, purple, bicolors**
Bloom Time: **Summer through fall**

Verbena is a spreading plant ideal for cascading over retaining walls, pots, baskets, and window boxes. As long as the soil is extremely well drained, verbena will reward gardeners with countless clusters of small blooms all season. It's fairly drought-tolerant, making it a great choice for hanging baskets, as well as rock gardens, planting in cracks between stones, and other tight places. One annual verbena, 'Imagination', is a standout for taking the hottest, driest conditions. It will even do well in a clay strawberry pot!

Varieties

1 'FUEGO RED'
Verbena 'Fuego Red' is a fast-growing variety that shows off big clusters of brilliant red flowers.

2 'SUPERBENA PINK PARFAIT'
Verbena 'Superbena Pink Parfait' shows off wonderful soft pink flowers over fuzzy, disease-resistant foliage. It grows 12 inches tall and up to 48 inches across, so it's ideal for a hortizonal container or a window box.

CONTAINER COMPANIONS

LARKSPUR
Larkspur's upright bloom spires look terrific when planted with sprawling verbena.

PETUNIA
Petunia and verbena colors coordinate well, and the contrast in bloom sizes is striking.

SNAPDRAGON
Use verbena to edge a container and back it up with cheerful snapdragons.

Zinnia
Zinnia selections

Type: **Annual**
Height: **1–4 feet tall**
Width: **1 foot wide**
Color: **White, orange, yellow, red, green, purple**
Bloom Time: **Summer through fall**

Want fast color for just pennies? Plant zinnias! A few seeds will fill a container with gorgeous flowers in an amazing array of shapes and colors, even green! And it will happen in just weeks. There are dwarf types of zinnias, tall types, quill-leaved cactus types, spider types, multicolored, special seed blends for cutting, special blends for attracting butterflies, and more. Zinnias are so highly attractive to butterflies that you can count on having these fluttering guests dining in your container garden every afternoon. But to attract the most, plant lots of red or hot pink zinnias in a large patch. 'Big Red' is especially nice for this, and the flowers are outstanding, excellent for cutting.

Varieties

1 'BENARY'S GIANT ORANGE'
Zinnia 'Benary's Giants Orange' is an excellent cut flower with large 4-inch-wide double orange blooms. It grows 38 inches tall and 2 feet wide, so plant it in a large container.

2 'PROFUSION WHITE'
Zinnia 'Profusion White' is an early-flowering selection with good disease resistance and white flowers all summer long. It grows 18 inches tall

TEST GARDEN TIP
Cut zinnias often for bright bouquets. Clipping flowers encourages more blooms.

CONTAINER COMPANIONS

SPIDER FLOWER
Spider flower makes an airy-looking backdrop behind the more solid-looking zinnia plants.

FRENCH MARIGOLD
Shorter, pure yellow marigolds such as 'Janie' or 'Lemon Gem' make charming companions.

SALVIA
'Victoria Blue' salvia holds its own when planted near zinnias. The cool blue color is a soothing transition between the bold hues of zinnias.

Alternanthera

Alternanthera selections

Type: **Annual, perennial, indoor plant**
Height: **6–36 inches tall**
Width: **6–18 inches wide**
Color: **Red, purple, or variegated foliage**
Bloom Time: **Foliage looks good from spring through fall.**

The two common names given to this tropical plant—calico plant or Joseph's coat—say it all: Its richly colored leaves in purples, bronzes, oranges, reds, purples, and yellows make it an exciting container candidate. In the tropics, it's a perennial, but most gardeners grow it as an annual. It's a top pick for containers, and if you have a sunny window, you can even bring it inside and use it as a houseplant. Like so many tropical plants, it likes rich, moist, but well-drained potting mix.

Varieties

1 JOSEPH'S COAT

Alternanthera ficoidea bears purplish foliage on a spreading low plant perfect for containers.

2 'GAIL'S CHOICE' JOSEPH'S COAT

Alternanthera 'Gail's Choice' offers dark purple-red foliage on an upright plant that can reach 3 feet tall.

CONTAINER COMPANIONS

ANGELONIA
Angelonia's richly colored upright flower spikes look great paired with variegated forms.

DUSTY MILLER
Go for the high-contrast look by combining a deep purple-red variety of alternanthera with the silvery foliage of dusty miller.

FOUNTAIN GRASS
Create a dark-on-dark look with an explosion of purple fountain grass foliage bursting out from a carpet of alternanthera.

Asparagus Fern
Asparagus selections

Type: **Annual, indoor plant**
Height: **18–36 inches tall**
Width: **18–36 inches wide**
Color: **White**
Bloom Time: **Foliage looks good from spring through fall.**

This subtropical relative of edible garden asparagus is in the lily family, but its needlelike foliage gives it an appearance resembling a fern. Its stems shoot up and outward, making it an excellent plant for hanging baskets. Give asparagus fern medium to bright indoor light and keep the soil uniformly moist. Plants sometimes develop small red berries, which are poisonous, so keep the berries away from children and pets.

Varieties

1 'MYERS'
Asparagus densiflorus 'Myers' has dense, bottle-brush-like stems that grow more upright. It makes a better tabletop plant than hanging basket.

2 'SPRENGERI'
Asparagus densiflorus 'Sprengeri', the most widely available variety, has arching stems with 1-inch-long dark green needles.

TEST GARDEN TIP
Trim off old stems to encourage new growth and to keep asparagus ferns looking fresh.

CONTAINER COMPANIONS

BLUE LOBELIA
Asparagus ferns offer a frilly cascade of green that complements the neon-blue flowers of lobelia.

SWEET ALYSSUM
Pair asparagus fern with lacy white sweet alyssum. The fern spills over the container's side and the sweet alyssum creates a frothy edge.

GERANIUM
Pink or red geraniums are great companions with asparagus ferns.

TEST GARDEN TIP

Begonias are extremely sensitive to frost. Cover them or take them indoors if temperatures dip.

Begonia
Begonia selections

Type: **Annual**
Height: **6–18 inches tall**
Width: **6–12 inches wide**
Color: **White, pink, red**
Bloom Time: **Summer through fall**

Talk about foolproof: Annual begonia is about as easy as it gets. It does well in a variety of conditions, but to enjoy it at its most luxuriant best, give it light shade; rich, well-drained soil; and ample water. It also loves plenty of fertilizer, so be generous. Protect containers planted with annual begonias in spring until after all danger of frost has passed. No need to deadhead this flower unless you want to; it's "self-cleaning"!

Varieties

1 'BELLAGIO APRICOT'
Begonia 'Bellagio Apricot' is a double-flowering begonia for shade with pendulous apricot flowers perfect for hanging baskets. It grows 14 inches tall and 2 feet wide.

2 'BONFIRE'
Begonia 'Bonfire' offers glowing orange flowers and narrow, bronzy-green leaves. It's especially effective in containers. It grows 20 inches tall and wide.

CONTAINER COMPANIONS

IMPATIENS
Combining white begonias with any color of impatiens is a surefire way to create a colorful display in a shady spot.

BLUE LOBELIA
Give white begonias a colorful skirt of blue lobelia for a stunning mix.

WISHBONE FLOWER
Wishbone flowers have a similar shape to begonias, so you can combine them to create an intriguing, subtle container display.

Cupflower
Nierembergia selections

Zones: **7–10**
Type: **Annual, perennial**
Height: **1 foot tall**
Width: **2 feet wide**
Color: **White, blue**
Bloom Time: **Summer through fall**

The adorable cup-shape flowers of nierembergia and its neat growth habit make it a useful annual flower for containers. Plant a row along the front edge of a planter or window box for a crisp look (especially the white-flowered varieties). It's also a great medium-height plant to visually tie together taller plants and cascading plants. Though it's usually grown as an annual, nierembergia is perennial in Zones 7–10.

Varieties

1 'AUGUSTA BLUE SKIES'
Nierembergia 'Augusta Blue Skies' is wonderfully heat- and drought-tolerant with lavender-blue flowers all summer long. It grows 12 inches tall and 24 inches wide.

2 'MONT BLANC'
Nierembergia 'Mont Blanc' is an award-winning variety with pure white flowers on an 8-inch-tall plant.

TEST GARDEN TIP
In extreme heat, make sure to water nierembergia well. It doesn't tolerate dryness.

CONTAINER COMPANIONS

SWEET ALYSSUM
Pair blue nierembergia with white sweet alyssum in containers for a colorful mound of flowers.

FLOWERING TOBACCO
White-flowering varieties of flowering tobacco are a perfect partner for nierembergia's mounding habit and charming blooms.

NIGELLA
Mix nierembergia's cup-shape flowers with the lacy, multipetal flowers of nigella for a long-blooming, charming combo.

TEST GARDEN TIP

In large containers, use dicondra as a creeping groundcover; pair with trees, shrubs, or standard roses.

Dichondra
Dichondra argentea

Zones: **9–11**
Type: **Annual**
Height: **2–6 feet long**
Width: **2 feet wide**
Bloom Time: **Foliage looks good from spring through fall.**

Dichondra's strands of soft small fan-shape leaves create a shimmering, cascade from hanging baskets and containers. A vigorous grower, it has runners that can grow as long as 6 feet and branch without pinching. The varieties 'Silver Falls' and 'Emerald Falls' combine especially well with purple and pink flowers. This heat- and drought-tolerant plant prefers slightly dry soil.

Varieties

1 *DICHONDRA ARGENTEA* **'SILVER FALLS'**
This striking new trailing annual gives you a fresh way to include elegant silver foliage in your container and other plantings. Perfect in a hanging basket, window box, or other container, this plant can trail up to 6 feet with showy, soft foliage like no other.

2 *DICHONDRA REPENS* **'EMERALD FALLS'**
'Emerald Falls' offers deep green leaves and a dense, symmetrical habit. The plant is very full and maintains a trim appearance.

CONTAINER COMPANIONS

ORNAMENTAL PEPPER
Create a bold contrast by planting purple-leafed peppers with 'Silver Falls' dichondra.

SAGE
Create an all-silver look with silver sage and dichondra. Both plants are also quite heat- and drought-tolerant.

VERBENA
Dichondra looks stunning paired with red or pink flowers such as verbena.

English Ivy
Hedera helix

Zones: **5–9**
Type: **Perennial**
Height: **2–4 feet long**
Width: **8–12 inches wide**
Bloom Time: **Foliage looks good all year.**

A woody-stemmed groundcover, English ivy trails gracefully over the edge of containers. Use the versatile vine to decorate a trellis or obelisk in a pot. Its lobed leaves may be solid green or variegated with white-and-green or green-and-yellow markings. Best grown in sun or partial shade, ivy eventually crowds out small, less-aggressive plants, so choose its companions wisely.

Varieties

1 'GLACIER'
Hedera helix 'Glacier' has bluish-green leaves washed with gray-green and white.

2 'NEEDLEPOINT'
Hedera helix 'Needlepoint' has medium green leaves with a long, narrow central lobe. Its deeply lobed leaves give the plant a fine texture.

TEST GARDEN TIP
Leave English ivy in window boxes all year. It tolerates cold to Zone 5 and provides green holiday decor.

CONTAINER COMPANIONS

EUGENIA
English ivy makes a great groundcover for formally clipped topiaries such as eugenia or rosemary.

BEGONIA
Plant with red, white, or pink begonias. Ivy makes a nice filler for a window box.

IMPATIENS
Interplant ivy with impatiens, a shade-tolerant annual. Ivy provides evergreen foliage all winter.

Eugenia
Eugenia selections

Zones: **10–11**
Type: **Perennial**
Height: **8 feet tall**
Width: **2 feet wide**
Color: **White**
Bloom Time: **Foliage looks good from spring through fall.**

Eugenia is a member of the myrtle family and features small glossy green leaves. This clippable tree is most often used as a topiary in container settings. Eugenias are usually available in garden centers in larger pots. They come in bush shape, which can be clipped into a cone form. A popular way to trim eugenias is in one-, two- or three-ball configurations.

Varieties

1 'LOLITA'
Eugenia uniflora 'Lolita' bears 1-inch, dark red fruit and dark green leaves.

2 'SURINAM CHERRY'
Eugenia uniflora 'Surinam Cherry' is also called Brazilian cherry, Cayenne cherry, and Florida cherry because this eugenia bears red fruit. Trees will fruit in a container.

CONTAINER COMPANIONS

AJUGA
Ajuga's green and coppery foliage makes an excellent base for topiary eugenia.

ENGLISH IVY
Add a frothy groundcover to topiary eugenia with a variegated English ivy.

PACHYSANDRA
The dark green foliage of perennial pachysandra makes an excellent groundcover for eugenia.

Euphorbia

Euphorbia selections

Zones: **2–11**
Type: **Annual**
Height: **3 feet tall**
Width: **2 feet wide**
Color: **White, variegated foliage**
Bloom Time: **Foliage looks good in spring, summer, and fall.**

If you'd like a low-maintenance annual for your containers (or beds and borders), it's tough to find a better performer than euphorbia. This group of plants offers outstanding heat and drought resistance. Plus, they have a white, milky sap that animals don't like, so they're rarely nibbled on by deer, rabbits, or other critters. (Be warned, though: The sap can irritate sensitive skin.) The wide variety of euphorbia selections offers different heights, colors, and textures.

Varieties

1 'DIAMOND FROST'
Euphorbia 'Diamond Frost' is one of the most popular container plants. A wonderfully heat- and drought-tolerant plant, it produces a continuous supply of frothy blooms from spring to fall. It grows 18 inches tall and 24 inches wide.

2 SNOW ON THE MOUNTAIN
Euphorbia marginata, or snow on the mountain, shows off green foliage that develops a white edge in late summer and fall. This self-seeding annual has clusters of white flowers at the end of the season and grows 3 feet tall and 1 foot wide.

TEST GARDEN TIP
Euphorbia 'Diamond Frost' can be brought indoors and used as a lacy foil to other houseplants.

CONTAINER COMPANIONS

ANGELONIA
Angelonia's purple, white, or pink flowers are perfect accents to 'Diamond Frost' euphorbia's frothy white flowers.

CORALBELLS
Purple, bronze, or chartreuse coralbells make a beautiful textural contrast to 'Helena's Blush'.

COSMOS
Cosmos, especially white selections, looks great with a planting of snow on the mountain.

Fuchsia

Fuchsia selections

Zones: **8–10**
Type: **Annual, perennial**
Height: **1–3 feet tall**
Width: **1–2 feet wide**
Color: **Pink, red, white, fuchsia, orange**
Bloom Time: **Summer through fall**

Exotic fuchsia is a fascinating flower, with lovely hanging lanternlike flowers in magentas, pinks, purples, and whites. If you're lucky, your fuchsia will attract hummingbirds. There are several types of fuchsia on the market. The most familiar to many gardeners are those grown in hanging baskets in the North. Recently, plant breeders have released a series of upright fuchsias with smaller flowers, often in shades of orange and red. Fuchsias are actually tender perennials grown as annuals outside tropical regions. Place them outside in spring after all danger of frost has passed. They need rich, well-drained soil and ample moisture.

Varieties

1 'BLACK PRINCE'
Fuchsia 'Black Prince' is a compact, upright variety that bears dark violet-and-red single flowers all summer long. It offers good heat tolerance and grows 2 feet tall and wide. Zones 8–10

2 'DARK EYES'
Fuchsia 'Dark Eyes' bears purple double flowers with cerise-red sepals on a plant that trails 2 feet and grows 30 inches wide. It tolerates heat well. Zones 8–10

TEST GARDEN TIP
Fuchsias do best in areas with cool summers; they don't like heat, humidity, or drought.

CONTAINER COMPANIONS

BROWALLIA
Complement hanging fuchsias with the star-shape blue flowers of browallia.

DICHONDRA
The bright foliage of 'Silver Falls' dichondra is the perfect way to set off a fuchsia, especially a dark-flowering type.

IMPATIENS
White impatiens look stunning with any fuchsia, and a white-on-white combination is especially lovely in the evening hours.

Gazania

Gazania selections

Zones: **8–10**
Type: **Annual, perennial**
Height: **1 foot tall**
Width: **1 foot wide**
Color: **Yellow, orange, cream, pink, white**
Bloom Time: **Summer through fall**

This tough plant endures poor soil, baked conditions, and drought easily and still produces bold-color, daisylike flowers from summer to frost. A perennial in Zones 9–11, gazania is grown as an annual in cooler regions and blooms from midsummer to frost. The flowers appear over toothed dark green or silver leaves (the foliage color differs among varieties). They're great in beds and borders as well as containers. Plant established seedlings outdoors after all danger of frost has passed.

Varieties

1 'DAYBREAK TIGER STRIPES MIX'
Gazania 'Daybreak Tiger Stripes Mix' bears yellow, pink, orange, and cream flowers with a contrasting band down each petal. It grows 10 inches tall.

2 'SUNBATHER'S SUNSET'
Gazania 'Sunbather's Sunset' offers amber-orange double flowers. It grows 18 inches tall and wide.

TEST GARDEN TIP
Do not fertilize gazanias; they do best without additional feeding. Keep soil on the dry side.

①

②

CONTAINER COMPANIONS

CALIFORNIA POPPY
Soften gazania's bold flowers with the delicate blooms of California poppy.

LISIANTHUS
Dwarf varieties of purple-flowering lisianthus look beautiful against gold and orange gazania varieties, especially those with fuzzy silver leaves.

PENTAS
Daisy-shape gazania flowers look beautiful against the full heads of pentas. Plus, butterflies love both plants.

TEST GARDEN TIP

Heucheras offer many types of brightly colored foliage; try several in a container for a surprising look.

Heuchera
Heuchera selections

Zones: **3–9**
Type: **Perennial**
Height: **2–3 feet tall**
Width: **6–30 inches wide**
Color: **Pink, red, white with colorful foliage**
Bloom Time: **Summer through fall**

Exciting new selections with incredible foliage patterns have put heucheras, also called coralbells, on the map. Previously enjoyed mainly for their spires of dainty reddish flowers, coralbells are now grown as much for the unusual mottling and veining of different-color leaves. The low clumps of long-stemmed evergreen or semi-evergreen lobed foliage make coralbells beautiful container plants. They enjoy humus-rich, moisture-retaining soil. Beware of heaving in areas with very cold winters.

Varieties

1 'DOLCE BLACKCURRANT'
Heuchera 'Dolce Blackcurrant' offers rich purple leaves with splashes of silver. It grows 16 inches tall and 20 inches wide. Zones 4–9

2 'DOLCE KEY LIME PIE'
Heuchera 'Dolce Key Lime Pie' features exciting lime green foliage from spring to fall and clusters of pink flowers in spring. It grows 16 inches tall and 14 inches wide. Zones 4–9

CONTAINER COMPANIONS

ASTILBE
The fluffy red, pink, or white flower plumes and ferny leaves of astilbe combine well with coralbells in shaded, moist sites.

HOSTA
Bold-foliage hostas prefer moist soil and somewhat shaded conditions, making them perfect partners for coralbells.

JAPANESE PAINTED FERN
The delicately variegated markings of Japanese painted fern echo the markings on coralbells.

Hydrangea
Hydrangea selections

Zones: **4–9**
Type: **Shrub**
Height: **3–6 feet tall**
Width: **3–4 feet wide**
Color: **Blue, pink, white, green, russet**
Bloom Time: **Summer through fall**

This shade-loving beauty offers huge bouquets of clustered flowers in various arrangements from mophead to lacecap from summer through fall. Varieties differ in size of plant and flower panicle, flower color, and blooming time. PeeGee turn russet and cling into winter. Oakleaf hydrangeas have the most handsome foliage, which reddens dramatically in fall. Some of the newer hydrangeas feature huge flowers on compact plants ideal for containers. Hydrangeas thrive in a moist, fertile, well-drained soil mix in partial to full shade. If you're seeking blue flowers, check your potting soil's pH level and apply aluminum sulfate in spring to lower pH. The change in flower color results from lower pH and higher aluminum content in the soil.

Varieties

1 'BLUE BUNNY' ('WIM RUTTEN')
Hydrangea involucrata 'Wim Rutten' is a reblooming lacecap with blue flowers from midsummer to frost. It grows 4 feet tall and 5 feet wide. Zones 6–9

2 OAKLEAF HYDRANGEA
Hydrangea quercifolia bears snowy cone-shape flowers in summer. Large leaves redden in fall. Grows 6 feet tall and 8 feet wide. Zones 5–9

TEST GARDEN TIP
To maximize the bloom season, choose hydrangeas that bloom on both the current and old growth.

CONTAINER COMPANIONS

VARIEGATED HOSTA
Try low-growing two-toned hostas to add a splash of light beneath a container hydrangea.

DOUBLE IMPATIENS
Combine pastel-hued double impatiens at the base of a pink, white, or blue hydrangea.

CALIBRACHOA
Small-flowered trailing calibrachoa look lovely spilling over the side of a hydrangea-filled container.

TEST GARDEN TIP

After it blooms in spring, shear back lobelia and it will likely rebloom in fall.

Lobelia

Lobelia selections

Zones: **2–11**
Type: **Annual**
Height: **1 foot tall**
Width: **1 foot wide**
Color: **Blue, white**
Bloom Time: **Spring through fall**

There are few blues more intense and gorgeous than those found on annual lobelia. The mounding type, called edging lobelia, is beautiful for planting in rows in containers and window boxes. The cascading type is stunning, like a sapphire waterfall spilling over the sides of pots. Annual lobelia is in its glory during the cool weather of spring and fall. Except for cool-summer areas, such as the Pacific Northwest or higher altitudes, lobelia stops flowering during the heat of summer.

Varieties

1 'RIVIERA MIDNIGHT BLUE'
Lobelia erinus 'Riviera Midnight Blue' bears dark blue flowers and bronze-tinged foliage on vigorous, mounding plants.

2 'LUCIA DARK BLUE'
Lobelia erinus 'Lucia Dark Blue' offers gorgeous true-blue flowers on a trailing plant that's more heat-tolerant than many older varieties. It trails to 24 inches.

CONTAINER COMPANIONS

LOOSESTRIFE
Mix blue lobelia with golden creeping Jenny for a bright, contrasting display to spill from a container or hanging basket.

DIANTHUS
Accent blue lobelia's beautiful flowers with brightly colored dianthus (and enjoy the scent from dianthus too).

PANSY
Grow blue lobelia as an edging in containers with blue, purple, or white pansies.

Mint

Mentha selections

Zones: **3–10**
Type: **Perennial, herb**
Height: **1–4 feet tall**
Width: **1–4 feet wide**
Color: **Flower color varies, but tends toward pastel or lighter shades.**
Bloom Time: **Foliage looks good from spring through fall.**

Plant a pot of cooling, refreshing fragrance by adding mint to your container garden. Undemanding and easy to grow, mint boasts a hearty constitution. Fragrance varies with variety, as does taste. Use mint fresh or dried to season a range of culinary creations including soups, beverages, vegetables, meats, and desserts. This herb releases scent when you crush or bruise leaves. Place it near garden paths or benches so you can savor the fragrance frequently. All mint varieties thrive in containers.

Varieties

1 PEPPERMINT
Mentha x *piperita* packs the strongest mint flavor. It grows 12–30 inches tall and 18 inches wide. Zones 3–8

2 VARIEGATED PINEAPPLE MINT
Mentha suaveolens 'Variegata' brightens up a large container with its white-edged leaves. This mint has a fruity flavor. It grows 3 feet tall and several feet wide. Zones 5–9

TEST GARDEN TIP
Include mint in your garden beds (but keep it from taking over) by planting it in a pot sunk into soil.

CONTAINER COMPANIONS

MINT
Plant a mint medley in a container using flavored mints such as chocolate, orange, and apple mint.

SWEET ALYSSUM
The frilly, lacy blooms of sweet alyssum look stunning next to the deep green leaves of mint.

BLUE LOBELIA
Deep green leaves of mint paired with the deep blue flowers of lobelia make a perfect pairing in containers. Tousle the mint to enjoy the fragrance.

TEST GARDEN TIP

Keep soil moist and fertilize lightly but regularly to keep New Guinea impatiens producing flowers.

New Guinea Impatiens

Impatiens selections

Type: **Annual**
Height: **1–2 feet tall**
Width: **1–2 feet wide**
Color: **Orange, white, pink, red, coral, bicolors**
Bloom Time: **Summer through fall**

Like their more common cousins, New Guinea impatiens provide hard-to-find brilliant color in shade. And it's not just the flowers. The foliage is often brilliantly, exotically colorful as well. These tropical plants really shine in containers, where they thrive in the perfect soil and drainage, but they also do well in the ground as long as you take the time to improve the soil and work in plenty of compost. They're a bit more sun-tolerant than common impatiens. Plant established plants in spring after all danger of frost has passed.

Varieties

1 'APPLAUSE ORANGE BLAZE'
Impatiens 'Applause Orange Blaze' bears bright orange flowers over variegated foliage. It's more cold-tolerant than many other varieties and grows 1 foot tall and wide.

2 'CELEBRETTE DEEP RED'
Impatiens 'Celebrette Deep Red' produces rich red flowers, which attract hummingbirds, over dark green foliage. It grows 10 inches tall.

CONTAINER COMPANIONS

DIANTHUS
Grow low varieties of dianthus with New Guinea impatiens for a colorful display all season.

IMPATIENS
While New Guinea impatiens tolerates sun, it also does fine in shade. Create a fun mix by planting New Guinea impatiens with mini impatiens.

SWEET POTATO VINE
In containers, dress up dark-leaf New Guinea impatiens with the bright foliage of chartreuse sweet potato vine.

Nicotiana
Nicotiana selections

Type: Annual
Height: 5 feet tall
Width: 2 feet wide
Color: White, green, pink, yellow
Bloom Time: Summer through fall

Many types of nicotiana are terrifically fragrant (especially at night) and are wonderful in attracting hummingbirds as well as fascinating hummingbird moths. This plant is also called flowering tobacco because it's a cousin of the regular tobacco plant. Try the shorter, more colorful types in containers and window boxes. These plants do best in full sun and moist, well-drained soil. Nicotiana may reseed.

Varieties

1 'NICKI RED'
Nicotiana 'Nicki Red' bears richly fragrant red flowers on 18-inch-tall plants.

2 'LIME GREEN'
Nicotiana 'Lime Green' bears chartreuse star-shape flowers on 2-foot-tall plants.

TEST GARDEN TIP
The taller, white-only types, which can reach 5 feet are ideal for night gardens; they require larger containers.

CONTAINER COMPANIONS

SPIDER FLOWER
Plant taller flowering tobacco varieties with cleome for a beautiful and airy display of white flowers that are perfect for evening gardens.

DUSTY MILLER
Contrast flowering tobacco's starry flowers with the silvery felted foliage of dusty miller for a great display all summer long.

FRENCH MARIGOLD
Old-fashioned marigolds look great with flowering tobacco in the ground or in containers.

TEST GARDEN TIP

Viola flowers are edible and add color to salads and desserts. Don't use pesticides if you plan to eat them.

Pansy
Viola selections

Zones: **2–11**
Type: **Annual, perennial**
Height: **4–9 inches tall**
Width: **4–12 inches wide**
Color: **Blue, violet, purple, white, yellow, cream, orange**
Bloom Time: **Spring through fall**

From tiny, cheerful Johnny jump-ups to the stunning 3-inch blooms of Majestic Giant pansies, the genus *Viola* has a spectacular array of delightful plants for the spring garden. They're must-haves to celebrate the first days of spring since they don't mind cold weather and can even take a little snow and ice! They're cherished for the early color they bring to pots, window boxes, and other containers. By summer, pansies bloom less and their foliage starts to brown. It's at this time that you'll have to be tough and tear them out and replant with warm-season annuals, such as marigolds or petunias. But that's part of their charm—they are an ephemeral celebration of spring!

Varieties

1 'BLUE & PURPLE RAIN'
Viola 'Blue & Purple Rain' is an award-winning selection with purple flowers that age to white, then mature to purple and blue. It grows 12 inches tall and 16 inches wide.

2 'BOWLES' BLACK'
Viola x *wittrockiana* 'Bowles' Black' offers purple blooms that are so dark they appear black.

CONTAINER COMPANIONS

ORNAMNETAL KALE
Kale and pansies can extend the bedding plant growing season for northern gardeners. They thrive in cool spring and fall temperatures and even withstand some frost.

OSTEOSPERMUM
Lavender osteospermum coordinate well with some of the lavender bicolor pansies.

SNAPDRAGON
Taller snapdragons make a great backdrop for shorter pansies.

Plectranthus

Plectranthus selections

Zones: **2–11**
Type: **Annual, perennial**
Height: **1–6 feet tall**
Width: **3–4 feet wide**
Color: **Green, green-and-white, green-and-gold, silver, purple foliage**
Bloom Time: **Foliage looks good from spring through fall.**

This vigorous foliage plant drapes neatly over container rims, making it ideal for window boxes, hanging baskets, and containers. Plectranthus is available with green or variegated foliage. Some varieites flower more than others. There's some plectranthus to complement any container planting. The foliage is also extremely fragrant.

Varieties

1 'MONA LAVENDER'
Plectranthus 'Mona Lavender' shows off rich purple leaves topped by spikes of lavender-purple flowers. It grows 28 inches tall and wide. It makes a lovely houseplant.

2 *PLECTRANTHUS ARGENTATUS*
Plectranthus argentatus displays hairy, silvery leaves and is easy to grow indoors or out. It grows 3 feet tall and wide.

TEST GARDEN TIP
Plectranthus makes a beautiful houseplant. Place in a sunny indoor location at the end of summer.

CONTAINER COMPANIONS

PETUNIA
Plectranthus provides the unique foliage, and petunias can provide the burst of color.

COLEUS, SHADE-LOVING
Plectranthus creates a miniature groundcover when planted at the feet of upright, bold-colored coleus.

OSTEOSPERMUM
Lavender osteospermum look lovely with purple-hued plectranthus such as 'Mona Lavender'.

TEST GARDEN TIP
Use well-drained soil for ranunculus; make sure containers have adequate drain holes.

Ranunculus

Ranunculus selections

Zones: 4–7
Type: **Bulbs**
Height: **12–14 inches tall**
Width: **12–14 inches wide**
Color: **White, red, yellow, orange, pink**
Bloom Time: **Spring, fall**

The flowers of ranunculus look as if they're made of crepe paper. Available in both single- and double-flowering varieties, blooms range in size from 1 to 4 inches wide. Most impressive are the double blooms, which are solidly packed with petals. Newer varieties offer the largest flowers and the full color range. Each ranunculus bulb produces six to eight flowers at intervals of one or two weeks, so you'll have lots of flowers for show and cutting.

Varieties

1 TECOLOTE 'RED'
Red ranunculus produce petal-packed flowers in spring. Bulbs produce more than 20 flowers.

2 'BUTTERED POPCORN'
'Buttered Popcorn' is a perennial ranunculus that produces bright yellow flowers on 12- to 15-inch-tall plants in late spring to summer. Zones 5–8

CONTAINER COMPANIONS

TULIPS
Spring-blooming bulbs such as tulips look stunning with cool-weather-loving ranunculus. Pair bright red tulips with yellow ranunculus.

PANSIES
Cool-weather-loving pansies create a frilly underplanting for taller ranunculus. Choose white or yellow pansies to create a fresh spring basket of blooms.

Sedge
Carex selections

Zones: **5–9**
Type: **Perennial**
Height: **6–30 inches tall**
Width: **6–30 inches wide**
Color: **Variegated white, yellow, green foliage**
Bloom Time: **Foliage looks good from spring to fall.**

Although it looks like an ornamental grass, most of which need full sun and thrive in hot, dry conditions, clump-forming sedge is completely different. For one thing, it's a sedge, not an ornamental grass. And it prefers shade along with moist soils (making it a great plant to tuck among hostas). Sedge's colorful arching foliage, most notably in beautiful glowing yellows, looks beautiful in a container alone or combined with flowering plants.

Varieties

1 'EVERGOLD'

Carex oshimensis 'Evergold', sometimes called *Carex hachijoensis*, is a low-growing plant with creamy yellow variegation. Zones 6–9

2 ISLAND BROCADE SEDGE

Carex ciliatomarginata 'Shima-nishiki' (also called Island Brocade *Carex siderosticha*), forms a dense groundcover with variegated leaves 6 to 9 inches long. Zones 5–8

TEST GARDEN TIP

Most sedges prefer moist soil and some midday shade in hot climates. Water every other day and fertilize monthly.

CONTAINER COMPANIONS

HOSTA
The bold foliage of hosta makes a dramatic contrast to the grassy foliage of sedges. Combine contrasting shades of green for added effect.

IRIS
The upright grasslike leaves of Siberian iris team well with the arching leaves of sedges. Both appreciate moist conditions and semishade.

TEST GARDEN TIP

Blue fescue produces seed heads that turn tan when mature. To keep plants tidy, clip them off.

Blue Fescue
Festuca glauca

Zones: **4–8**
Type: **Perennial**
Height: **6–10 inches tall**
Width: **6–10 inches wide**
Color: **Blue foliage**
Bloom Time: **Spring through fall**

One of the most versatile ornamental grasses, blue fescue can be used in containers as a centerpiece—it makes a fabulous fountain of foliage. Blue fescue is evergreen in all but its northernmost range. The fine bluish foliage looks best when it is fresh in spring and early summer.

Varieties

1 'ELIJAH BLUE'
Festuca glauca 'Elijah Blue' forms a compact 8- to 10-inch-tall tuft of fine bluish-green leaves. Zones 4–8

2 'SEA URCHIN'
Festuca glauca 'Sea Urchin' is also sometimes listed by its official name 'Seeigel'. It forms a dense 10-inch-tall mound. Zones 4–8

CONTAINER COMPANIONS

DIANTHUS
The blue-green foliage of dianthus closely matches that of fescue. Top it off with pink blooms and you've got a dynamite combination.

BLANKET FLOWER
Mounds of gold, orange, and maroon daisies of blanket flower team superbly with the spiky bluish mounds of blue fescue foliage.

SHRUB ROSE
Blue fescue makes an attractive groundcover at the base of a rose bush.

Bromeliad

Aechmea, Alcantarea, Ananas, Cryptanthus, Guzmania, Neoregelia, Tillandsia selections

Zones: **10–11**
Type: **Perennial**
Height: **Varies by species**
Width: **Varies by species**
Color: **Green, red, pink, purple, yellow**
Bloom Time: **Summer**

Blushing bromeliads are low-maintenance tropicals that make colorful, easy-care houseplants. The plants have a rosette of serrated straplike leaves that form a cup in the center. Immature foliage is green, often striped with white or chartreuse, but when the plant is about to flower, the leaves develop a rosy hue, giving rise to the common name of blushing bromeliad. Small purple flowers develop in the cup, but they're secondary to the colorful leaves. Other bromeliads offer a variety of flower shapes and hues.

Varieties

1 'RAPHAEL' BLUSHING BROMELIAD
Neoregelia 'Raphael' blushing bromeliad has deep green leaves with a narrow white margin.

2 'STARLIGHT'
Aechmea 'Starlight' bears coral blooms and green, glossy spineless leaves.

TEST GARDEN TIP
Keep blushing bromeliads well hydrated—just pour water into the central vase of leaf bases.

CONTAINER COMPANIONS

RED PEPPER
The fiery red peppers on hot pepper plants are a wonderful mixer with bromeliads.

BANANA
The giant leaves of banana, especially red-tipped varieties, look great with bromeliad to deliver a container with a tropical punch.

CROTON
Beautiful tropical croton leaves come in a wide variety of splotchy colors that meld nicely with colorful bromeliads.

TEST GARDEN TIP

Tubers can be overwintered indoors and moved outdoors once temperatures stay above 60°F.

Caladium

Caladium selections

Zones: **10–11**
Type: **Bulb**
Height: **8–20 inches tall**
Width: **24 inches wide**
Color: **Cream, pink, red, silver, green foliage**
Bloom Time: **Foliage looks good from late spring through fall.**

Providing color pizzazz in dim places where flowers can't, caladiums have come into their own recently with the craze for tropical plants. The clumping, heart-shape leaves are available in a variety of veined patterns in many colors. Newer introductions bring caladiums out of the shade. The more substantial leaves of the Florida series, with greater heat tolerance, give the splashy caladiums their place in the sun. They look stunning in containers alone or combined with bright blooming annuals.

Varieties

1 'FLORIDA CARDINAL'
Caladium 'Florida Cardinal' produces red heart-shape leaves broadly bordered in green. The plant grows 12 inches tall and is part of a thicker-leaved caladium series bred in Florida for sun tolerance. Zones 10–11

2 'FLORIDA ELISE'
Caladium 'Florida Elise' bears vibrant splashes of silvery pink that highlight the 16-inch-long leaves. This variety takes more sun than most and grows 2 feet tall. Zones 10–11

CONTAINER COMPANIONS

OTHER CALADIUMS
Plant several bulbs with different-colored foliage in the same large container.

ELEPHANT'S EAR
Large leafy elephant's ear looks great with lower-growing caladiums creating a flounce of color beneath them in a container.

BEGONIA
Shade-loving begonias in ruby red or clear pink are excellent mixers with complementary-colored caladiums.

Coleus

Solenostemon hybrids

Zones: **2–11**
Type: **Annual**
Height: **1–4 feet tall**
Width: **1–3 feet wide**
Color: **Red, green, white, burgundy, pink foliage**
Bloom Time: **Foliage looks good from spring through fall.**

Add excitement to dim areas of your yard with shade- and sun-loving coleus varieties. An amazing array of color combinations is available, as well as leaf textures—choose from plants with scalloped, toothed, or fringed leaf edges. Trailing shade-loving coleus is an easy-to-grow annual foliage plant that adapts well to hanging baskets and container gardens where its sprawling stems can drape over the edge of the planter.

Varieties

1 'TELLTALE HEART'
Solenostemon 'Telltale Heart' has heart-shape leaves with scalloped green edges and a deep purple-maroon center. It is slow to flower, so it needs little pinching or pruning to maintain its trailing shape. It trails to 18 inches.

2 'ATLAS'
Solenostemon 'Atlas' is a stocky shade-tolerant foliage plant with purplish maroon leaves splashed with a contrasting bright green center. The bright green color is repeated in a narrow band edging each leaf. It grows 2 feet tall.

TEST GARDEN TIP
Take cuttings of coleus at the end of summer. Root in water or use rooting hormone and plant in potting soil.

CONTAINER COMPANIONS

SOLID-COLOR COLEUS
Solid-color shade-loving coleus grows well even in the darkest corners if you give it water, a little fertilizer, and wait to site containers outdoors until after the weather is consistently warm. Solid-hued leaves mix well with multicolored varieties.

BEGONIA
Shade-loving begonias in ruby red mix well with complementary-colored coleus. Both love shaded locations.

Croton

Codiaeum variegatum pictum

Zones: **10–11**
Type: **Perennial**
Height: **1–6 feet tall**
Width: **1–3 feet wide**
Color: **Yellow, green, pink**
Bloom Time: **Foliage looks good all year.**

Croton is a colorful shrublike plant with leathery leaves that are most colorful in bright shade. They add instant structure and loads of color when placed in the center of a large container. In denser shade conditions new leaves will be smaller and less intensely pigmented. Grow croton at 60°F to 85°F with high humidity.

Varieties

1 'ANDREW'

Codiaeum variegatum pictum 'Andrew' is variegated with a wavy creamy yellow band around its leaf margin and a two-tone gray-green central leaf body.

2 'RED ICETON'

Codiaeum variegatum pictum 'Red Iceton' has foliage that emerges yellow or chartreuse and gradually turns gold with a wash of red.

CONTAINER COMPANIONS

NEW GUINEA IMPATIENS
Tall-growing crotons enjoy an underplanting of coordinating colorful New Guinea impatiens. Both species do well in shade.

BROMELIAD
Spiky, colorful bromeliads look smashing with painterly croton varieties.

Elephant's Ear
Alocasia selections

Zones: **7–11**
Type: **Bulb**
Height: **3–7 feet tall**
Width: **3–7 feet wide**
Color: **Green, white, bronze, maroon**
Bloom Time: **Foliage looks good from summer through fall.**

Elephant's ears are big, dramatic, tropical-looking plants grown for their bold foliage. Aptly named, many bear triangular leaves that are leathery and uniquely textured. They grow well in large containers and can also be grown indoors as houseplants. The clumping foliage adds lush effects on porches and patios. Plants sprout from large bulbous roots and achieve maximum growth in warm, humid summer temperatures.

Varieties

1 AFRICAN MASK PLANT
Alocasia amazonica is an exotic foliage plant featuring large, leathery arrowhead leaves in shades of olive green, bronze, or maroon. It grows 3 feet tall. Zones 9–11

2 'PURPLE PRINCE'
Alocasia grandis 'Purple Prince' features 2- to 3-foot stems topped with gorgeous, glossy white-veined leaves.

TEST GARDEN TIP
Unpot and store these large bulbs at the end of the season. You can replant them next spring.

CONTAINER COMPANIONS

COLEUS
For an all-foliage festival, combine color forms of coleus with the leafy charms of elephant's ear.

CALADIUM
Large and colorful caladiums look stunning with equally impressive elephant's ear. Plant together in a large colorful container and enjoy the textural interplay of the massive leaves.

TEST GARDEN TIP

Plant false cypress in containers to add a formal look to patios and porches.

False Cypress
Chamaecyparis selections

Zones: **5–9**
Type: **Tree**
Height: **2–3 feet tall**
Width: **2–3 feet wide**
Color: **Green, light green, silver, blue foliage**
Bloom Time: **Foliage looks good all year-round.**

Incomparable texture and color intensity make false cypress a valuable companion in containers. Group them together to create an attractive hedge or screen. The fanlike boughs hold long, soft needles that resemble filigreed lace or ferns. The upswept branches of Hinoki cypress look like a Japanese painting, while the Nootka false cypress features pendulous branches. Color range of the false cypress extends from blue-gray to deep green to gold. A moist, slightly acidic soil is ideal for these trees; they do not thrive in hot and dry or windy conditions.

Varieties

1 'BABY BLUE'
Chamaecyparis pisifera 'Baby Blue' is a compact selection that forms a dense shrub of silvery-blue foliage. It grows 6 feet tall and 4 feet wide. Zones 4–8

2 'CRIPSII'
Chamaecyparis obtusa 'Cripsii' features golden foliage that deepens to dark green. Zones 4–8

CONTAINER COMPANIONS

DWARF ARBORVITAE
Go for a textural twofer by combining dwarf arborvitae with false cypress.

MONEYWORT
The golden-yellow, coinlike leaves of moneywort look beautiful as an underplanting for false cypress.

DWARF ALBERTA SPRUCE
Dark green and soft needled, dwarf Alberta spruce make nice container companions for false cypress.

Ferns
Many species

Zones: **3–10**
Type: **Perennial**
Height: **1–2 feet tall**
Width: **1–2 feet wide**
Color: **Green or variegated foliage**
Bloom Time: **Foliage looks good from spring through fall.**

Graceful, lacy fronds add textural intrigue—and sometimes gray-green coloration—to container plantings. Whether upright or arching, ferns make elegant companions to more colorful growers such as impatiens, begonias, and coleus. Use beautiful maidenhair ferns to add an airy, delicate texture in shade garden containers. Maidenhair ferns are lovely when grouped in a shady, moist, well-drained location, forming a fine-textured mass. One of the most elegant ferns available for containers, Japanese painted ferns are washed with gorgeous silver and burgundy markings. Lady fern is equally elegant though not quite as showy.

Varieties

1 JAPANESE PAINTED FERN
Athyrium niponicum pictum is one of the best-known ferns. Its silvery fronds tinged with burgundy make an elegant container or garden accent. Zones 5–8

2 AMERICAN MAIDENHAIR FERN
Adiantum pedatum is native to North America and bears upright black or brown stalks with featherlike medium green fronds. It grows 12–16 inches tall. Zones 3–8

TEST GARDEN TIP
Fill a pair of urns or other traditional containers with large ferns to create instant ambience.

CONTAINER COMPANIONS

HOSTA
The bold foliage of hosta provides a dramatic contrast to the finely divided fronds of maidenhair fern.

BEGONIA
Pink, white, and red begonias add colorful highlights to dark green fern fronds.

COLEUS
Splashy coleus are colorful companion for ferns. Use pink- and chartreuse-hued coleus to brighten up fern-filled containers.

TEST GARDEN TIP

Plant this showy grass in large containers with other grasses such as blue fescue for a fresh look.

Hair Grass

Deschampsia caespitosa

Zones: **4–9**
Type: **Perennial**
Height: **1–2 feet tall**
Width: **1–2 feet wide**
Color: **Green foliage**
Bloom Time: **Foliage looks good from spring through summer.**

Tufted hair grass gets its name from the fine, hairlike flowers that rise about the plant. They emerge green and turn shades of gold, forming clouds that look like a beautiful, unruly head of golden hair. A native to damp woods, bogs, and streamsides, tufted hair grass prefers a cool spot in partial shade.

Varieties

1 'TARDIFLORA' TUFTED HAIR GRASS
Deschampsia cespitosa 'Tardiflora' blooms in late summer with greenish clouds of flowers over a mound of medium green foliage. Zones 4–9

2 'NORTHERN LIGHTS', VARIEGATED HAIR GRASS
Deschampsia caespitosa 'Northern Lights' is a green grass with creamy white variegation. Enjoy this nice touch: Leaves turn pink in cold weather. Zones 4–9

CONTAINER COMPANIONS

LIGULARIA
Ligularia appreciates moist soil, as does tufted hair grass. Its coarse mound of foliage makes a dramatic contrast to the airy cloud of tufted hair grass blooms.

PRIMROSE
Primroses are great for adding brilliant color around the base of tufted hair grass. They also appreciate partial shade and moist potting mix.

Hosta
Hosta selections

Zones: **3–9**
Type: **Perennial**
Height: **5 feet tall**
Width: **4 feet wide**
Color: **Green, white, cream, yellow, blue foliage; flowers are white or lavender**
Bloom Time: **Midsummer**

This plant, hardly grown 40 years ago, is now one of the most common garden plants. But hosta has earned its spot in the hearts of gardeners—it's among the easiest plants to grow, as long as you have some shade and ample rainfall. Hostas vary from tiny plants suitable for troughs or small containers to massive 4-foot clumps with heart-shape leaves that can fill large containers or baskets.Leaves can be puckered, wavy-edged, white or green variegated, blue-gray, chartreuse, emerald-edged—the variations are virtually endless.

Varieties

1 'BLUE MOUSE EARS'
Hosta 'Blue Mouse Ears' is a charming dwarf selection with rounded blue leaves. It grows 5 inches tall and 12 inches wide. Zones 3–9

2 'AZTEC TREASURE'
Hosta 'Aztec Treasure' has 1-foot mounds of heart-shape chartreuse leaves and bell-shape purple flowers in summer. Zones 3–8

TEST GARDEN TIP
Use hosta's white or purplish flowers in cut flower bouquets.

CONTAINER COMPANIONS

ASTILBE
Astilbe and hosta is the classic partnership in shaded places. The fine astilbe foliage and colorful flower plumes complement hosta leaves.

HOLLY FERN
The upright fronds of Christmas fern contrast well against the solid foliage of hosta in shade.

COLUMBINE
The dancing, colorful flowers of columbine bloom when hostas are beginning to unfurl their young leaves.

TEST GARDEN TIP
Impatiens wilt rapidly in hot weather; frequent watering is a must.

Impatiens
Impatiens selections

Type: **Annual**
Height: **1–2 feet tall**
Width: **1–2 feet wide**
Color: **White, pink, fuchsia, orange, yellow**
Bloom Time: **Summer through fall**

What would we do without impatiens? It's the old reliable for shade gardens when you want eye-popping color all season long. The plants bloom in just about every color except true blue and are well suited to growing in containers or in the ground. If you have a bright spot indoors, you may be able to grow impatiens all year as an indoor plant.

Varieties

1 'SUPER ELFIN WHITE'
Impatiens 'Super Elfin White' bears pure-white flowers on compact, 10-inch-tall plants.

2 'FUSION INFRARED APRICOT'
Impatiens 'Fusion Infrared Apricot' bears apricot-pink flowers with yellow-orange throats. It grows 16 inches tall.

CONTAINER COMPANIONS

BROWALLIA
Mix blue browallia with pink, white, or lavender impatiens for a steady show of soft color all the way to fall.

BEGONIA
Big, beautiful tuberous begonias are a great accent to impatiens, especially double-flowering impatiens.

WISHBONE FLOWER
Create subtle textural contrast by mixing wishbone flowers with impatiens plantings.

Japanese Maple
Acer selections

Zones: **3–9**
Type: **Tree**
Height: **3–15 feet**
Width: **10–12 feet**
Color: **Red, green, chartreuse, burgundy, variegated foliage**
Bloom Time: **Foliage looks good from spring through fall.**

Elegant Japanese maples make excellent container plants. Most have an exquisitely layered, cascading form, fine leaf texture, and remarkable fall color. Among the many varieties, there are maples with yellow-green, purple, red, bronze, and variegated leaves. And their sizes suit containers. They vary from 3-foot dwarfs to slow-growing 15-footers.

Varieties

1 'BENI SCHICHIHENGE'
Acer palmatum 'Beni Schichihenge' bears green leaves edged in pink and cream. They turn shades of yellow in fall. This tree grows 8 feet tall and wide. Zones 6–9

2 'DISSECTUM ATROPURPUREUM'
Acer palmatum 'Dissectum Atropurpureum' bears broad, arching branches with finely textured reddish-purple leaves. It grows 8 feet tall and 10 feet wide. Zones 6–8

TEST GARDEN TIP
Japanese maples don't like wind, so position them in a protected location.

CONTAINER COMPANIONS

HOSTA
The bold foliage of hosta provides a dramatic contrast to the finely divided leaves of Japanese maples.

BEGONIA
Pink, white, and red begonias add colorful highlights to chartruese-hued Japanese maples.

LAMIUM
Splashy white-and-green lamium make colorful companions for Japanese maples.

Jacob's Ladder
Polemonium selections

Zones: **4–9**
Type: **Perennial**
Height: **1–3 feet tall**
Width: **6 inches to 2 feet wide**
Color: **White, pink, blue, lavender, yellow; variegated leaves**
Bloom Time: **Spring and early summer**

Jacob's ladder is a favorite native plant for shady spots. It has handsome long leaves, sometimes variegated, with a ladderlike arrangement of leaflets. Heavy clusters of clear lavender-blue, pink, yellow, or white flowers with conspicuous stamens nod atop slender stems. Jacob's ladder is a winner in sunny or lightly shaded areas; place containers on porches or patios that receive dappled light.

Varieties

1 'STAIRWAY TO HEAVEN'
Polemonium reptans 'Stairway to Heaven' bears pink-and-white-edged leaves and lavender-blue flowers in early summer. It grows 2 feet tall. Zones 3–7

2 'BRIZE D'ANJOU'
Polemonium caeruleum 'Brize D'Anjou' is not as floriferous as many others, but its leaves are dramatically rimmed with creamy white. It grows 2 feet tall. Zones 4–9

CONTAINER COMPANIONS

CORALBELLS
The dainty spires of red or pink coralbells are fine companions for Jacob's ladder in light shade.

PHLOX
Creeping phlox has flattish flowers in pinks, blues, and white that mix well with those of blue Jacob's ladder in light shade.

CANDYTUFT
The dark leaves and dramatic white flower heads of perennial candytuft provide a strong foil for Jacob's ladder in sun.

Moneywort
Lysimachia nummularia

Zones: **3–10**
Type: **Perennial**
Height: **1–2 feet long**
Width: **2 feet wide**
Color: **Light green foliage**
Bloom Time: **Foliage looks good from spring through fall.**

Moneywort, also called creeping Jenny, forms a dense green mat that cascades over the edges of containers. It's especially nice in window boxes. This easy-care perennial produces a bounty of long, slender stems covered with dime-size leaves. Bright yellow cup-shape blooms emerge in summer to fall. Although plants may bloom, the foliage packs the biggest punch with this creeping beauty.

Varieties

1 GOLDEN CREEPING JENNY
Lysimachia nummularia 'Aurea' is a fast-growing groundcover for shade or partial shade. It bears round chartreuse foliage and grows 2 inches tall. It can spread indefinitely. Zones 4–8

2 CREEPING JENNY
Lysimachia nummularia offers creeping green foliage that forms a dense mat. Fast-growing, it reaches just 2 inches but spreads quickly.

TEST GARDEN TIP
Moneywort requires consistently moist soil to look its best. Keep it well hydrated.

CONTAINER COMPANIONS

BLACK MONDO GRASS
The spiky black foliage of black mondo grass contrasts nicely with the creeping habit and chartreuse foliage of moneywort.

COLEUS
Pair moneywort with purple and red varieties of coleus. The color combination is easy and eye-catching.

HOSTA
Variegated hosta varieties are lovely pot mates with moneywort.

TEST GARDEN TIP

Most oxalis selections do best in part to full shade and well-drained soil. Be sure not to overwater.

Oxalis

Oxalis selections

Zones: **6–11**
Type: **Annual, perennial, bulb**
Height: **12 inches tall**
Width: **12 inches wide**
Color: **White, lavender, yellow flowers; red, purple, green and yellow foliage.**
Bloom Time: **Foliage looks good from spring through fall.**

Also known as shamrock plant and wood sorrel, oxalis features a trio of heart-shape green or purple leaves that may be marked with black or silver. This easy-to-grow charmer works both indoors and out. Oxalis bears colorful, cloverlike leaves that close up at night. They appear in a range of colors from silver to purple—and several are variegated with other colors. The cup-shape blooms are also attractive.

Varieties

1 'MOLTEN LAVA'
Oxalis vulcanicola 'Molten Lava' produces stunning orange-chartreuse foliage and decorative golden-yellow flowers all spring and summer. It grows 10 inches tall and wide. Zones 9–11, or try it as a houseplant.

2 'IRON CROSS'
Oxalis tetraphylla 'Iron Cross' offers leaves divided into four leaflets. The center of each is decorated with a purple blotch that looks great against the pink flowers. It grows 10 inches tall and wide. Zones 8–9, though it also thrives as a houseplant.

CONTAINER COMPANIONS

HOSTA
The wavy, heart-shape leaves of hosta make an excellent planting friend to oxalis, especially the purple-leafed types.

SEDUM
Pair low-growing sedums, such as 'Dragon's Blood', with oxalis to create a colorful container for shady spots.

DAFFODILS
Small, spring-blooming daffodils look so perky rising out of a bed of leafy oxalis.

Persian Shield
Strobilanthes dyerianus

Zones: **9–10**
Type: **Annual, perennial**
Height: **2–3 feet tall**
Width: **2 feet wide**
Color: **Burgundy foliage**
Bloom Time: **Foliage looks good from spring through fall.**

Persian shield's purple foliage shimmers with hints of green and silver on top, while the leaves' underside is solid maroon. The plant's large, showy, almond-shape leaves deliver lots of pizzazz in a container.

Use this lofty grower to add height to a pot. It's a natural centerpiece plant. It grows 2 to 3 feet tall; as the main plant in a container, it commands attention. Also nice is that its rich and dramatic color can be seen from far away.

Plant with chartreuse-leafed or white-flowering companions to make the purple leaves really pop.

Persian shield needs moisture and should be watered often; don't allow the soil to dry out. You can enjoy this showy plant indoors. If keeping Persian shield as a houseplant, mist several times a week.

TEST GARDEN TIP
Pinch back Persian shield early in the growing season and you'll get thicker, bushier foliage.

CONTAINER COMPANIONS

COLEUS
Mix and match chartreuse and purple coleus with the leafy talents of Persian shield.

LAMB'S-EARS
The soft, silvery leaves of lamb's-ears look lovely with the colorful leaves of Persian shield.

IMPATIENS
Underplant pink-tinged Persian shield with a layer of pink impatiens for a perfect-in-pink combination.

Polka-Dot Plant

Hypoestes phyllostachya

Zones: **10–11**
Type: **Annual, perennial**
Height: **10–12 inches tall**
Width: **9 inches wide**
Color: **White, red, pink, green foliage**
Bloom Time: **Foliage looks good spring through fall.**

The spotted foliage of polka-dot plant is marked with white, red, or pink dots, making it a gorgeous foliage plant for containers. This plant thrives in cramped quarters and humid conditions, preferring moist, rich soil. Water every other day and give a monthly feeding. Polka-dot plant has a tendency to get leggy, especially in deep shade. To encourage tidy growth, pinch stem tips, remove the flower spikes, and provide morning sun.

Varieties

1 WHITE POLKA-DOT PLANT
Large pointed green leaves are splashed with bright white splotches. Plants grow 12 inches tall and 9 inches wide.

2 PINK POLKA-DOT PLANT
Pretty green leaves are heavily blotched with pink so that from afar, the leaves look almost all pink. This plant loves moist soil.

CONTAINER COMPANIONS

HOSTA
Large-leafed, single-color hostas combine well with the small, splashy leaves of polka-dot plant.

COLEUS
Create a color fantasy in a container with pink-hued coleus and polka-dot plant.

IMPATIENS
Interplant pink impatiens with polka-dot plant for a beautiful pastel shade-loving combination.

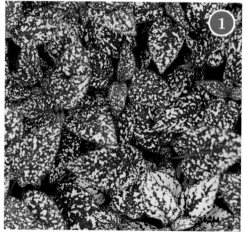

Spotted Dead Nettle

Lamium maculatum

Zones: **4–8**
Type: **Perennial**
Height: **6–12 inches tall**
Width: **6–12 inches wide**
Color: **Pink, white, lavender; silver-, white-, or yellow-variegated foliage**
Bloom Time: **Late May to early summer**

A fast-growing groundcover, spotted dead nettle makes a showy statement spilling over the sides of a container. After the first bloom, cut stems back to encourage more compact growth and avoid self-sowing.

Varieties

1 'BEACON SILVER'

Lamium maculatum 'Beacon Silver' has thick whorls of purple-pink two-lip flowers from spring through fall if deadheaded routinely and not allowed to desiccate. The small triangular leaves are mostly silver with a bright green edge. Zones 4–8

2 'HERMAN'S PRIDE'

Lamium galeobdolon 'Hermann's Pride' is more compact than the species. Its serrated leaves are crisply splashed with silver between the veins. In spring, whorls of yellow two-lip flowers bloom. Zones 4–8

TEST GARDEN TIP
Lamium can take more sunshine in cool climates. Set containers in partially shaded areas.

CONTAINER COMPANIONS

WILD GINGER
In shade, evergreen European wild ginger forms low mats of glossy kidney-shape leaves that contrast well with the spotted dead nettle foliage.

LILYTURF
In spring, the grasslike silver-and-white striped leaves of 'Silver Dragon' lilyturf add striking contrast to the leaves of spotted dead nettle.

HEART-LEAF BRUNNERA
Blue-flowering brunnera produce clumps of heart-shape foliage that look lovely with *Lamium*.

TEST GARDEN TIP

Prune vinca regularly to keep in check; stems that reach the ground will root.

Vinca

Vinca minor

Zones: **4–11**
Type: **Perennial**
Height: **3 feet long**
Width: **6 inches wide**
Color: **White, lavender**
Bloom Time: **Spring**

Vinca, also called periwinkle, is a fast-growing groundcover that is prized as a trailer for containers and window boxes. In spring it produces 1-inch-wide funnel-shape flowers. The leaves of variegated types combine light and dark green, white, or yellow. Vinca does best in part shade. Some vincas sold for pots are the species *Vinca major,* which is hardy only to Zone 7.

Varieties

1 PURPLE VINCA
Vinca minor 'Atropurpurea' bears creeping stems and dark purple flowers on and off from spring to fall. Zones 4–9.

2 VINCA MINOR
Vinca minor offers pretty blue blooms periodically from spring to frost. Zones 4–9.

CONTAINER COMPANIONS

LUNGWORT
The silver-spotted hairy leaves of lungwort make an interesting contrast with dark evergreen periwinkle in shaded places.

LILYTURF
Variegated lilyturf has upright clumps of strappy green leaves edged with cream, which show off well among the dark foliage of vinca in light shade.

Wishbone Flower

Torenia fournieri selections

Zones: **10–11**
Type: **Annual, perennial**
Height: **8–12 inches tall**
Width: **6–9 inches wide**
Color: **Yellow, purple, white, lavender**
Bloom Time: **Spring through fall**

Just peek inside the two-lipped flowers and you'll see where the name comes from. Wishbone flower is also called clown flower. From planting to frost this showy flower brightens shady areas with a profusion of blooms. These undemanding heat- and humidity-tolerant plants maintain a glorious show without deadheading.

Varieties

1 'CATALINA GILDED GRAPE'

Torenia fournieri 'Catalina Gilded Grape' is a mounding selection featuring bright yellow flowers with purple throats. It grows 16 inches tall and trails 24 inches.

2 'CATALINA WHITE LINEN'

Torenia fournieri 'Catalina White Linen' shows off lovely pure white flowers on a compact, mounding/trailing plant. It grows 16 inches tall and 24 inches across.

TEST GARDEN TIP
Keep wishbone flower in top shape by feeding every two weeks with a potassium-rich fertilizer.

CONTAINER COMPANIONS

SWEET ALYSSUM
Sweet alyssum in white or pastel shades combines well with the color spectrum offered by wishbone flower.

BEGONIA
Fibrous-rooted begonia with white blooms and bronze foliage looks great planted at wishbone flower's feet.

IMPATIENS
Wishbone flower shines among a planting of impatiens in solid pink or white.

TEST GARDEN TIP

Regular watering is key to sustaining the black-eyed Susan vine's vigorous growth.

Black-Eyed Susan Vine

Thunbergia alata

Type: **Annual**
Height: **8 feet long**
Width: **2 feet wide**
Color: **Yellow, white, orange**
Bloom Time: **Summer through fall**

Dark-eyed, vibrant flowers nestle among black-eyed Susan vine's soft green leaves. Support this clambering vine with a trellis in a container to put its height to work. Or leave it on its own to cascade over the sides of the container. Black-eyed Susan vine looks great intertwining with other vines on a trellis in a large container.

Varieties

1 'SUNNY LEMON STAR'
Thunbergia alata 'Sunny Lemon Star' offers big yellow flowers with brown centers. It climbs to 8 feet. Zones 10–11, but it's usually grown as an annual.

2 'LITTLE SUSIE'
Thunbergia alata 'Little Susie' bears white flowers with a chocolate-purple center. It climbs to 8 feet. Zones 10–11, but it's usually grown as an annual.

CONTAINER COMPANIONS

ZINNIAS
Narrow-leaf white-flowered zinnias with bright yellow centers make a great base planting for black-eyed Susan vine.

'LADY IN RED' SALVIA
'Lady in Red' is an award-winning, long-blooming, heat- and drought-resistant salvia with bright red flowers that look stunning planted at the base of a trellis covered with black-eyed Susan vine.

Clematis

Clematis selections

Zones: **4–9**
Type: **Perennial**
Height: **4–30 feet**
Width: **4–30 feet**
Color: **White, yellow, pink, purple, blue, red, burgundy, bicolors**
Bloom Time: **Summer through fall**

Clematis is undoubtedly the most versatile vine you can grow. Few other climbers offer such a broad range of bloom colors, shapes, and seasons. Dwarf clematis are great for growing in containers or along decks and patios.

Varieties

1 'BEE'S JUBILEE'
Clematis 'Bee's Jubilee' is a compact selection with deep pink flowers banded with red. It blooms in late spring and early summer and climbs to 8 feet tall. Zones 4–9

2 'DUCHESS OF EDINBURGH'
Clematis 'Duchess of Edinburgh' puts on a show with double white flowers in early summer with a repeat performance in late summer. This heirloom clematis grows 8 feet tall. Zones 4–9

TEST GARDEN TIP
The best clematis for containers are the compact varieties— those that grow to under 12 feet tall.

CONTAINER COMPANIONS

PETUNIA
Plant upwardly mobile clematis in a container with cascading petunia.

SWEET ALYSSUM
Plant an all-white container with white clematis 'Duchess of Edinburgh' with a lacy flounce of sweet alyssum at the base.

GOLDEN CREEPING JENNY
The green-yellow, dime-size leaves of golden creeping Jenny contrast nicely with blue-flowering clematis.

Cypress Vine

Ipomoea quamoclit

Type: **Annual**
Height: **20 feet**
Width: **20 feet**
Color: **Red**
Bloom Time: **Midsummer to frost**

Cypress vine is undoubtedly one of the lovliest annual vines because it has beautiful foliage and flowers. This vigorous vine has finely cut large leaves accented with an abundance of trumpet-shape scarlet flowers. Another added benefit of this vine: Hummingbirds adore the sweet nectar from the blooms.

Cypress vine is closely related to morning glory; like its relative, the flowers open in the early part of the day and close in the afternoon. But even after the flowers have closed up shop, you'll enjoy its feathery, finely cut foliage.

Use cypress vines in containers with a trellis or train the vine onto a nearby post or building. This annual reseeds, so you may enjoy the vine again next season.

Start cypress vine from seed in early spring. Or you can find already-started seedlings at local garden centers or through mail-order sources.

CONTAINER COMPANIONS

GERANIUM
Red, pink, or white geraniums look stunning with the bright red flowers of cypress vine.

MORNING GLORY
Intertwine a blue- or white-flowered morning glory vine with a cypress vine for a colorful container planting on a trellis.

PETUNIAS
Fill in the base of a trellis-clad cypress vine in a container with a cascade of frothy white petunias.

Honeysuckle Vine

Lonicera selections

Zones: **4–9**
Type: **Perennial**
Height: **25 feet**
Width: **25 feet**
Color: **Yellow, pink, orange**
Bloom Time: **Spring through fall**

Hummingbirds adore honeysuckle vine, and after growing one you will too. These easy-care climbers offer attractive clusters of blooms in a wide range of shades. The tube-shape flowers look great mixed in with a variety of shrubs, perennials, and annuals.

Varieties

1 'DROPMORE SCARLET'
Lonicera x *brownii* 'Dropmore Scarlet' bears slightly fragrant crimson-red flowers all summer long. It climbs to 12 feet. Zones 4–9

2 'GOLD FLAME'
Lonicera 'Gold Flame' is a strongly growing vine with fragrant orange-yellow flowers all summer. It climbs to 15 feet. Zones 6–9

TEST GARDEN TIP
Watch for hummingbirds around the tubular blooms of honeysuckle vine— they love it.

CONTAINER COMPANIONS

VERBENA
Underplant honeysuckle vine with a layer of cascading yellow or pink verbena.

OTHER HONEYSUCKLE VINES
Plant two containers of honeysuckle and space them about 4 feet apart. Back them with a trellis and allow the two container plants to grow up onto the trellis and intertwine.

TEST GARDEN TIP

Use hyacinth bean vine in containers to create a wall of foliage and flowers. Train onto a vertical trellis.

Hyacinth Bean Vine

Dolichos lablab

Type: **Annual**
Height: **8 to 10 feet**
Width: **8 to 10 feet**
Color: **Lavender**
Bloom Time: **Summer through fall**

Hyacinth bean offers fragrant bright purple flowers all summer. The spires of flowers are borne on long stems. This vigorous vine is a great choice to create a large container filled with foliage and flowers.

Plant two containers with hyacinth bean vine seedlings and connect them with a trellis. The vines will grow up and over to create an archway of foliage and flowers.

The bright purple blooms transform into stunning shiny burgundy-purple seedpods. (The seeds are easy to collect and store over winter.)

Although the flowers of this annual vine are so distinctive, the foliage is also showy. It's usually tinged with purple.

Start hyacinth bean vine from seed in early spring. Or you can find already-started seedlings at local garden centers or through mail-order sources.

CONTAINER COMPANIONS

MORNING GLORY
Intertwine purple-flowering hyacinth bean vine with varieties of blue- or white-flowering morning glory.

VERBENA
Plant purple verbena at the base of a container of hyacinth bean vine for a double dose of purple color.

Jasmine
Jasminum selections

Zones: **6–10**
Type: **Perennial shrub, vine**
Height: **15 feet or more**
Width: **15 feet or more**
Color: **White, yellow**
Bloom Time: **Early spring**

Few vines rival jasmine for beauty and fragrance. This easy-to-grow climber produces beautiful clusters of starry flowers you can smell from several feet away. Most jasmines bloom in late winter or early spring, but some, such as Arabian jasmine, will flower throughout the year. Most jasmines do best in full sun or part shade and moist, well-drained soil rich in organic matter.

Varieties

1 COMMON JASMINE
Jasminum officinale is a vigorous woody vine with fragrant white flowers from summer to fall. It can climb 35 feet or more. Zones 9–10

2 WINTER JASMINE
Jasminum nudiflorum is the hardiest jasmine. It's a shrub with yellow flowers in late winter and early spring. Unlike most jasmines, it is not fragrant. Useful as a hedge, it grows 10 feet tall and wide. Zones 6–9

TEST GARDEN TIP
If you love your jasmine, bring it indoors. It can live as a houseplant indoors in a sunny location.

CONTAINER COMPANIONS

VERBENA
Plant white-flowering verbena at the base of a container with jasmine vine. The verbena will cascade downward as the jasmine climbs upward.

CALIBRACHOA
Add a skirt of dusty blue calibrachoa to a potted jasmine. The blue and white color combination is soothing and refreshing.

TEST GARDEN TIP
Don't overwater your mandevilla. Too much water results in yellow or dropping leaves.

Mandevilla
Mandevilla selections

Zones: **10–11**
Type: **Annual, perennial**
Height: **20 feet**
Width: **20 feet**
Color: **Pink, white, red**
Bloom Time: **Summer through fall**

Among the garden's most elegant vines, mandevilla offers stunning trumpet-shape flowers. It grows great in containers; it's usually sold in large containers already trained onto a small trellis. If you want a lush, tropical look, this easy tropical plant is a must. Mandevilla is usually grown as an annual, though it can be overwintered indoors in a bright spot.

Varieties

1 'SUN PARASOL CRIMSON'
Mandevilla 'Sun Parasol Crimson' bears intense crimson-red blooms on a semibushy plant that can reach 15 feet. Zones 10–11

2 CHILEAN JASMINE
Mandevilla laxa bears fragrant white flowers in summer and early autumn. It climbs to 15 feet. Zones 10–11

CONTAINER COMPANIONS

CALIBRACHOA
Pair bright pink calibrachoa with pink mandevilla for a container that grows in both directions—up and away and cascading downward.

JASMINE
Intertwine a fragrant jasmine vine with a scentless mandevilla and you get the best of both worlds: beautiful flowers and intoxicating fragrance.

Moonflower Vine

Ipomoea alba

Zones: **10–11**
Type: **Annual, perennial**
Height: **15 feet**
Width: **15 feet**
Color: **White**
Bloom Time: **Late summer through fall**

Moonflower is a simply stunning and romantic flower. This easy-to-grow tropical vine is a close relative of the morning glory. It is named moonflower because its 6-inch-wide pure-white flowers unfurl only after sunset. This ideal evening-garden plant's large trumpet-shape flowers open in the evening and bloom until the sun rises. During the day, moonflower vines are studded with beautiful long, twisted buds.

Beauty is just one appealing aspect of the bloom. Fragrance is the other. The open flowers are deeply scented—which is a hidden secret of this vigorous vine.

While treated as an annual in most areas, it will grow as a perennial in frost-free climates. Moonflower climbs 15 feet or more and grows best in full sun.

This vine is commonly confused with another plant called moonflower. That plant, *Datura meteloides*, is not a vine, though it produces similar flowers that are also fragrant and open in the evening.

CONTAINER COMPANIONS

MORNING GLORY

Plant morning glory vines to intertwine with moonflowers so you can enjoy morning glory flowers during the day and moonflowers in the evening.

MINIATURE ROSES

Cluster a group of miniature roses beneath the vines of moonflower. You'll have flowers and fragrance during the day and moonflower's disklike fragrant flowers in the evening.

TEST GARDEN TIP
Try moonflower vine in containers in night gardens. Their white blooms and lovely fragrance are an asset.

TEST GARDEN TIP

Morning glories can self-seed and "replant" themselves for next season.

Morning Glory
Ipomoea selections

Type: **Annual**
Height: **15 feet**
Width: **15 feet**
Color: **White, red, blue, pink, purple, yellow, bicolors**
Bloom Time: **Summer through fall**

This fast-growing annual vine is a perfect pick for creating privacy on large container-based trellises during the summer. It produces a profusion of trumpet-shape flowers that open in the morning and usually close by afternoon. Morning glory is an annual that frequently reseeds, so you may enjoy the same variety next season as it replants itself.

Varieties

1 'HEAVENLY BLUE'
Ipomoea 'Heavenly Blue' is a classic variety with sky blue flowers. It climbs to 12 feet.

2 'SCARLETT O'HARA'
Ipomoea 'Scarlett O'Hara' bears bright reddish-pink blooms with delicate white throats. It climbs to 15 feet.

CONTAINER COMPANIONS

OTHER MORNING GLORY VARIETIES
Plant multiple morning glory vines on one trellis to intertwine the bloom colors. Try dark purple 'Grandpa Ott' or blue-striped 'Glacier Blue'.

PETUNIA
Plant double petunias at the base of a morning glory on a trellis to create a layer of flowers and foliage at ground level.

Crocus

Crocus selections

Zones: **3–8**
Type: **Bulb**
Height: **2–6 inches tall**
Width: **1–3 inches wide**
Color: **White, pink, lavender, purple, yellow, bicolors**
Bloom Time: **Spring**

Often poking up through the last drifts of snow, crocuses are one of the opening acts of the spring-bulb show. Their large cup-shape blooms appearing in tufts of grasslike foliage create magical plantings in baskets and small spring containers. They thrive in any well-drained soil in full to partial sun.

Varieties

1 'BOWLES WHITE'
Crocus sieberi 'Bowles White' bears snowy, chalice-shape flowers with deep yellow throats in early spring. It grows 2–3 inches tall. Zones 3–8

2 'LILAC BEAUTY'
Crocus tommasinianus 'Lilac Beauty' offers lilac-blue flowers that gradually open to reveal showy, divided gold stamens. Flowers abundantly in early spring on plants that grow 2 inches tall. Zones 3–8

TEST GARDEN TIP
Crocus looks stunning planted amid grass in containers; they make charming springtime centerpieces.

CONTAINER COMPANIONS

SCILLA
Petite scilla, also a spring-blooming bulb, is a great mate for Easter egg-colored crocus in early spring planters.

PANSIES
Cool-weather annuals such as yellow, blue, or white pansies are easy to tuck in amid blooming crocus.

DAFFODILS
Small daffodils such as 'Tete-a-Tete' are excellent companions with multicolored or yellow crocus.

Daffodil
Narcissus selections

Zones: **3–9**
Type: **Bulb**
Height: **6–20 inches tall**
Width: **4–6 inches wide**
Color: **White, pink, tose, yellow, gold, orange, bicolors**
Bloom Time: **Spring**

Cheery daffodils are one of the first risers in the spring garden. They are extremely easy to force and look stunning in baskets with other early spring risers, such as crocus and muscari. Daffodils stand up to cool weather (including frost snaps) and thrive best in spring. Hot, dry weather causes the blooms to fade quickly, so move containers to a protected location if this type of weather occurs.

Varieties

1 'PEEPING TOM'
Narcissus 'Peeping Tom' is an old-fashioned variety with a long yellow trumpet and slightly recurved yellow petals. It blooms in early to midspring on stems 6–12 inches tall. Zones 3–9

2 'TETE A TETE'
Narcissus 'Tete a Tete', whose name is French for "head-to-head" or "face-to-face," gets its moniker from its clusters of one to three flowers borne on petite 6- to 8-inch-tall stems. The bright yellow blooms appear in early spring. Zones 3–9

TEST GARDEN TIP
Once daffodils fade in containers, move them to the garden, where they may return next year.

CONTAINER COMPANIONS

VIOLA
Purple, blue, and yellow violas are excellent partners with daffodils. Both love cool weather and will bloom their hearts out all spring.

PRIMULA
Low-growing, cool-weather primula come in a wide variety of pastel bloom colors that look beautiful with yellow and white daffodils.

Muscari
Muscari selections

Zones: **3–8**
Type: **Bulb**
Height: **3–8 inches tall**
Width: **3–8 inches tall**
Color: **Blue, purple, white, yellow**
Bloom Time: **Spring**

Grape hyacinths add perky blooms and the sweet scent of grape bubblegum as well. These easy-care bulbs are frequently mass-planted to create a river effect in borders—and you can do the same thing in containers.

Varieties

1 'BLUE SPIKE'
Muscari armeniacum 'Blue Spike' is a selection in which each flower protrudes from the spike for a bristly, double-flower effect. This variety grows 8 inches tall. Zones 4–8

2 *MUSCARI LATIFOLIUM*
Muscari latifolium is distinguished by the single broad leaf wrapped around the tall stem. The flower spike is a two-tone mixture of open lavender bells above tight blue buds. The plant grows 6 inches tall. Zones 4–9

TEST GARDEN TIP
To keep muscari blooming longest, set containers in a cool area of the yard.

CONTAINER COMPANIONS

CROCUS
The deep blue hues of muscari blend well with white and yellow crocus. Crocus' grasslike foliage adds nice texture.

VIOLA
Cool-weather-loving blue, lavender, and yellow violas are a match made in heaven when paired with blue muscari.

IVY
Ivy creates a lovely cascading flow of green foliage around the base of blooming muscari.

Scilla

Scilla siberica

Zones: **2–8**
Type: **Bulb**
Height: **6 inches tall**
Width: **3 inches wide**
Color: **Blue, purple, white**
Bloom Time: **Early spring**

This hardy European native gives spring containers one of the loveliest shades of blue. The intense azure blossoms are held in loose spikes. Look closely to see the dark blue veins running down the flowers and the blue anthers that protrude from each blossom. Like the later-blooming grape hyacinths, squills are most impactful when planted in large groups (because they are such small bulbs). Plant in a large container for the best color effect. Scilla bloom for 2–3 weeks in early spring and have a light, pleasing fragrance.

Varieties

1 'SPRING BEAUTY'
Scilla 'Spring Beauty' delivers truly blue flowers for spring containers. Plant in fall and enjoy in spring. Zones 4–8

2 EARLY SCILLA, WHITE SQUILL
Scilla mischtschenkoana is also called early scilla or white squill. This lighter-blooming scilla offers star-shape flowers that resemble little bells. Zones 4–8

CONTAINER COMPANIONS

TULIPS
Low-growing species tulips come up in early spring just as scilla is starting to bloom. Pair bright-hued species with electric blue scilla.

CROCUS
Chalice-shape blooms of crocus contrast nicely with the pendulous, bell-shape flowers of scilla.

DAFFODILS
Create a spring basket of bloom with white, yellow, or orange trumpeted daffodils mixed amid a thick layer of scilla.

Tulip
Tulipa selections

Zones: **3–8**
Type: **Bulb**
Height: **4–14 inches tall**
Width: **6 inches wide**
Color: **White, red, pink, purple, lavender, yellow, coral, green, orange, bicolors**
Bloom Time: **Spring**

If you want long-lived tulips, pick the species types. These include wild varieties and selections developed from those species. Most are smaller in stature and bloom size than hybrid tulips, so they are perfect for containers. Because they are variants of wildflowers, species tulips are usually long-lived, hardy, and withstand spring weather conditions. Many open only in sunny conditions, keeping their blooms closed on cloudy days or in the evening.

Varieties

1 'HENRY HUDSON'
Tulipa vvedenskyi 'Henry Hudson' was a new tulip introduciton in 2009. This orange-red variety is an early to midspring bloomer on stems 6–10 inches tall. The blue-green leaves have crimped, wavy edges. It makes a great addition to patio planters or as a focal point in the front of a border. Zones 3–8

2 'HONKY TONK'
Tulipa clusiana 'Honky Tonk' is sometimes called lady tulip or candlestick tulip. It's a low-growing variety, reaching only 8 inches tall. Its blooms are all yellow on the inside but blushed with peach on the outer petals. Zones 3–8

TEST GARDEN TIP
Low-growing species tulips are ideal for spring containers. They can take spring's cold snaps with grace.

CONTAINER COMPANIONS

DAFFODILS
Choose short, multistemmed daffodils such as 'Tete a Tete' to pair with tulips.

SCILLA
Electric blue scilla is low growing and a perfect pairing for red or yellow tulips.

CROCUS
Challice-shape blooms of crocus look lively at the feet of taller tulips. Pair yellow and light blue crocus with pink tulips to create an Easter basket of early spring blooms.

The USDA Plant Hardiness Zone Map

Each plant has an ability to withstand cold temperatures, called a hardiness rating. This range of temperatures is expressed as a zone. A zone map shows where you can grow any specific plant.

Planting for Your Zone

There are 11 zones from Canada to Mexico, and each zone represents the lowest expected winter temperature in that area. Each zone is based on a 10-degree difference in minimum temperatures. Once you know your hardiness zone, you can choose plants for your garden that will flourish. Look for the hardiness zone on the plant tags of the perennials, trees, and shrubs you buy.

Microclimates in Your Yard

Not all areas in your yard are the same. Depending on your geography, trees, and structures, some spots may receive different sunlight and wind and consequently experience temperature differences. Take a look around your yard and you may notice that the same plant comes up sooner in one place than another. This is the microclimate concept in action. A microclimate is an area in your yard that is slightly different (cooler or hotter) than the other areas of your yard.

Create a Microclimate

Once you're aware of your yard's microclimates, you can use them to your advantage. For example, you may be able to grow plants in a sheltered, southern-facing garden bed that you can't grow elsewhere in your yard. You can create a microclimate by planting evergreens on the north side of a property to block prevailing winds. Or plant deciduous trees on the south side to provide shade in summer.

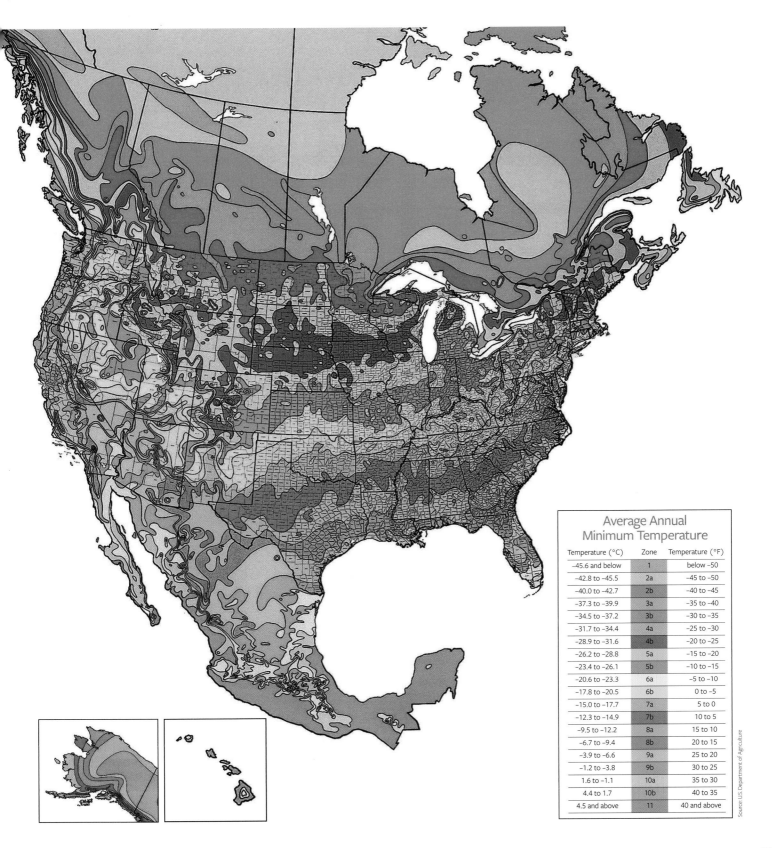

Average Annual Minimum Temperature

Temperature (°C)	Zone	Temperature (°F)
−45.6 and below	1	below −50
−42.8 to −45.5	2a	−45 to −50
−40.0 to −42.7	2b	−40 to −45
−37.3 to −39.9	3a	−35 to −40
−34.5 to −37.2	3b	−30 to −35
−31.7 to −34.4	4a	−25 to −30
−28.9 to −31.6	4b	−20 to −25
−26.2 to −28.8	5a	−15 to −20
−23.4 to −26.1	5b	−10 to −15
−20.6 to −23.3	6a	−5 to −10
−17.8 to −20.5	6b	0 to −5
−15.0 to −17.7	7a	5 to 0
−12.3 to −14.9	7b	10 to 5
−9.5 to −12.2	8a	15 to 10
−6.7 to −9.4	8b	20 to 15
−3.9 to −6.6	9a	25 to 20
−1.2 to −3.8	9b	30 to 25
1.6 to −1.1	10a	35 to 30
4.4 to 1.7	10b	40 to 35
4.5 and above	11	40 and above

Source: U.S. Department of Agriculture

Index

Page numbers in bold indicate the Encyclopedia entry for that plant. Numbers in italics indicate photographs.